A WAY
TO VICTORY

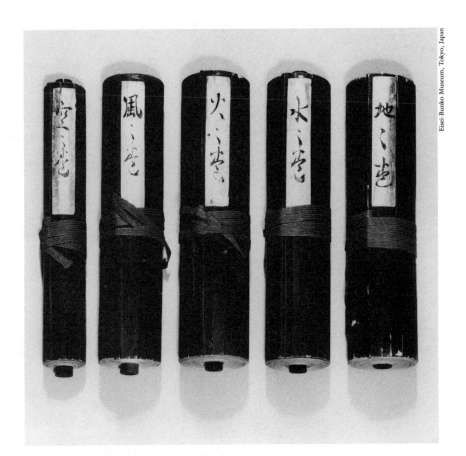

Five scrolls titled "Gorin no sho" by Miyamoto Musashi

A WAY TO VICTORY

THE ANNOTATED
BOOK OF FIVE RINGS

TRANSLATION AND COMMENTARY BY
HIDY OCHIAI

THE OVERLOOK PRESS
Woodstock & New York

First published in the United States in 2001 by
The Overlook Press, Peter Mayer Publishers, Inc.
Lewis Hollow Road
Woodstock, NY 12498
www.overlookpress.com

Library of Congress Cataloging-in-Publication Data

Miyamoto, Musashi, 1584-1645
    [Gorin no sho. English]
    A way to victory : the annotated Book of five rings/ [translated by]
    Hidy Ochiai.
    p. cm.
    Includes bibliographical references.
    ISBN 1-58567-038-3
    1. Military art and science –Japan—Early works to 1800. 2.
    Swordplay—Japan—Early works to 1800. I. Ochiai, Hidy. II. Title.

U101.M5913 2000
355.02—dc21   00-027016

Manufactured in the United States of America

ISBN 1-58567-038-3

1 3 5 7 9 8 6 4 2

CONTENTS

PART I

ABSOLUTE VICTORY

WINNING AND SUCCESS

Let us imagine a hypothetical situation: you're about to present a creative idea at an important meeting. If your idea is accepted by the people at the meeting, it would be a tremendous feather in your cap, which should help you at the time of your next promotion. However, suppose that there is someone else who is also thinking or presenting his idea about the same subject as yours at the meeting, hoping that others will accept his proposal instead of yours. In other words, it is either your idea or his. In such a case, for you to achieve your immediate objective, you must "defeat" the other person. Although there is no physical violence involved, of course, the situation is metaphorically akin to that of a combat between two warriors in the samurai age of Japanese history. It is mental combat and you must win at any cost without resorting to illegal or unethical tactics.

Winning strategy in combat is described by Miyamoto Musashi, one of the most famous and accomplished samurai warriors, in *The Book of Five Rings*.[1] For Musashi, one of the most vital elements in winning is the concept of *sen*[2] described in *Fire*, the third of five sections in *The Book of Five Rings*. *Sen* refers to a mental and physical method of dominating the opponent by using superior timing to win. So, applying the concept of *sen* to the hypothetical situation described above, you should try to find an opportunity to start speaking as soon as the meeting begins. At the time when people are not properly prepared for the meeting and before anyone else has a chance to open his or her mouth, you must present your idea with full vigor and confidence, in such a way that others will be overwhelmed by the force of your presentation. By mastering the situation by superior timing, you'll be in a better position to get the others to agree with you and accept your brilliant idea first. The other person, who was planning to present his idea, won't have a chance to open his mouth or, if he does, will be in the difficult position of having to change the minds of those who have thrown their support behind your idea.

On the other hand, if your rival speaker has started to speak before you, according to the application of Musashi's strategy, let him speak. Concentrate on his presentation, and as you listen to him intently, at the moment he stumbles or hesitates in his speech, or at the moment when you find some error, inconsistency, or weakness, jump right in and stop him. A decisive, powerful counter-argument made at the right time will "destroy" the other person's presentation. Once you succeed in making others aware of the flaw or weakness in the opponent's presentation, you can go ahead with your own speech and convince others to appreciate the validity and uniqueness of your idea.

As will be demonstrated in this book, Musashi was a great psychologist as well as a superb sword fighter. Among many mental strategies he shares in *The Book of Five Rings* is an interesting one called *utsuraseru*,[3] which means "to let others catch." He explains that yawning and sleepiness are catching, for example. If you pretend that you are sleepy and tired and act with a sluggish attitude, others around you will come to feel the same way. This mental technique can be used effectively in competitive situations such as sports.

A successful application of the concept of "catching" was made by a college football coach who, a couple of hours before an important game, had his players deliberately appear relaxed and nonchalant. He told them to shout and be rowdy and act as if they didn't care about the outcome of the game at all. Watching these players act as if they weren't prepared to play, the other team's members became confused. They didn't know what to make of the opposing team's curious behavior. They then became less serious about the game and their "fighting spirit" was less intense as they caught the relaxed and nonchalant attitude of the other team.

Something extraordinary happened. As soon as the game started, the team that had acted as if it didn't care at all about the game and was considered the underdog, came on with full concentration, fighting spirit, and focus. The other team didn't have a chance to recover its mental preparedness. The tactic of "catching" worked. The first team, led by the coach who followed the old warrior's teaching, became victorious against the odds, demonstrating that the essence of strategy in winning is basically the same in modern-day sports as it was among samurai warriors in seventeenth-century Japan.

Musashi's keen observation of human society includes the idea of overcoming difficult situations that we all encounter in life. He states that these times require extra effort and a determined attitude. He explains that it is like the situation of a ferryman who has to sail a boat. The ferryman may encounter difficult moments such as unexpected bad weather, rapids, or a particularly long stretch which he must overcome in order to complete the intended course. It requires an extra amount of determination, concentration, and effort in order to succeed. Such crucial moments can be found in all facets of human life. They can be found in our lives in general, in sports, in our careers, or in a simple trip. Even during an ordinary day, if observed carefully, there are some moments when we have to be more focused on certain matters than other times, since these moments require extra energy, patience, effort, and determination to pass through.

Regarding the methods of observing things and people, Musashi stresses the difference between *kan* and *ken*.[4] For example, most of us have a tendency to judge a person by how he or she dresses. There is actually nothing wrong in making a judgment of some sort based on the clothes that one wears, for there is a certain meaning in it. However, Musashi warns us that we should not be deceived by physical appearance. It is important for us to cultivate the ability to understand a person or thing in more ways than that which our physical eyes can judge. Perception into things or people that goes beyond a mechanical or physical seeing is called *kan*, while everyday seeing by the physical eyes is called *ken*.

If one does not apply the *kan* method of seeing, he or she can easily misjudge people or things. For example, when I was about sixteen years old, I visited a different dojo (martial arts school)[5] at my teacher's recommendation. When I arrived at the entrance of the new dojo, there was no one around to whom I could hand over the letter of introduction from my teacher. I went around the building to the backyard, where I saw an old man of small stature sweeping the yard. When I saw him, I spontaneously bowed down to him, but not with a feeling of particular respect, for I did not think he was a person of high position. I was much embarrassed later when I learned that the old man was head of the dojo. It was due to lack of my ability of *kan* that I made an error in judgment.

By using *kan*, I should have observed properly who the old man was through his absolutely balanced posture, the eyes demonstrating inner strength and the peaceful attitude that could have been attained only by a person of the ultimate achievement in martial arts—a true master. A superficial seeing through physical eyes, which is *ken*, needs no particular training. But a true understanding of a person or a thing requires *kan*, which is based on the focus of mind, wisdom, as well as intuitive knowledge. In order to acquire the ability for *kan*, one needs to pay special attention to observe something beyond what his or her physical eyes can see and use constant effort to strengthen the mind.

Today, when there are so many gimmicks and tricks to impress or deceive others in many facets of society, the importance of *kan* is obvious to all, but most people use *ken* in their lives, due mainly to habit and lack of ability for *kan*. For example, there was once a very large national open karate championship that was held in a large city in the U.S. It was when the sport of karate was still in a young stage in America, and all styles, traditional and nontraditional alike, competed together. This particular event was produced by an able promoter and drew many well-known karate figures from all over the U.S. and Canada.

Before the actual competition started, many people were betting on who would be the winner of the tournament. The competitors were warming up in a large open space which could be seen by the audience. All the reporters and camera people surrounded a few special competitors with flashy uniforms who were performing spectacular movements and exciting the audience. Everyone thought that the winners of that day would be some of those competitors who were drawing the most attention.

But there was a small Oriental-looking man who was quietly performing stretching exercises alone in the corner. No one paid any particular attention to him. He wore a regular traditional white *gi* (training uniform) and was not doing anything special that would deserve attention from others. But, by the end of the tournament, all eyes had shifted to this small man, whose performance throughout the tournament amazed everyone. Those who were showing off to the audience with spectacular movements before the tournament did not even survive the eliminations. People were deceived by the flashy uniforms and meaninglessly "spectacular" movements by the competitors, who might also have fooled themselves into believing that they might be the winners.

The Book of Five Rings is remarkable in many ways. Despite the fact that it was written in the middle of the seventeenth century and in feudal Japan, it still contains many precious ideas that we can apply to our daily lives in the modern world. Theories and techniques described in the book are based on the author's personal experiences of numerous life-and-death battles. Strategy and tactics are born out of the author's realization of the highest stage of the way of sword fighting. In the beginning, the way of the sword was a mere survival method for Musashi, but toward the end of his life, it became the basis of self-actualization: a form of enlightenment.

There were other classical documents written by other masters of sword fighting in almost the same period as Musashi, but in many cases, these masters used abstract language derived from books on Buddhism and Confucianism. Some of the authors even claimed that they had been given the secret techniques of the fighting arts by unknown forest-dwelling beings or mysterious creatures from the sea or rivers. In other words, by using unclear terms and difficult language, the authors seem to have tried to give the impression that their own styles of fighting were special and superior.

Miyamoto Musashi specifically mentions in the beginning of *The Book of Five Rings* that he deliberately avoided using old words from the laws and scriptures of Buddhism and Confucianism. As a result, the book is relatively easy to understand and remarkably refreshing for a work written in the middle of the seventeenth century by a samurai who spent most of his life as a *ronin* (masterless samurai).

It's true that Musashi intended to teach his readers to be victorious in one-to-one combat as well as in war involving armies. But if you read the book carefully, with an open mind and sincere attitude, it becomes clear that Musashi's teaching goes far beyond that. His philosophy can be summarized as *ji-riki*: the power of each individual that emanates from within oneself. Musashi believed that *ji-riki* must be cultivated and empowered through constant effort and training. With correct understanding, his messages become concrete and personal, directly relating to the problems of living—to the human being who struggles and strives for individual achievement. It's truly a teaching that transcends time, place, and culture.

If we want to actualize our potential greatness as human beings, we must be willing to make an effort. As Musashi himself demonstrates, the important things are constant training, self-discipline, and perseverance to make the best and most of the true self. We must believe that we can emerge as victors in life. Musashi is an example of a self-actualized person, who is free and authentic, capable of doing anything and becoming whatever he wants to be by using his self-power.

Practical strategies and fighting tactics necessary to win in combat are truly profound, according to Musashi, so much so that once you delve into the very foundation of these strategies and tactics, you can find fundamental principles common to all human endeavors. It is no wonder, then, that Musashi's book is still valued today as a guide to achieving success in the business and industrial worlds of Japan and the Western nations.

The days of everyday battles to the death were over a long time ago. We live in a civilized world, where all human beings should strive to live in peace and harmony. Musashi's theory of triumphing over others, therefore, should be interpreted as a constructive method of overcoming challenges in life, personal or otherwise, and actualizing our greatest possible potential so that we can become positive contributors to the world.

The Book of Five Rings is a gift from an old warrior to those who aspire to make the most and best out of their lives.

A BIOGRAPHICAL SKETCH OF MIYAMOTO MUSASHI

There is a small village called Miyamoto Mura located in the northeastern part of Okayama prefecture. Ben-no-suke, as Musashi was called in childhood, was born in this village in the twelfth year of the Ten-sho Era (1584). His father, Muni-sai, was an accomplished martial artist in his time. Although Musashi himself claims in *The Book of Five Rings* that he did not need a teacher or guide of any kind, it is certainly likely that Muni-sai had an influence on the young Musashi regarding the world of martial arts. It's also likely that the young Musashi's introduction to the world of fighting strategy was made through observation of his father's solo practice in the yard. There is no denying that Musashi was endowed with a certain gift for fighting strategy, which was further developed through his own extraordinary effort and determination, and the fact that his father happened to be a capable martial artist.

According to a book called *Tanji-Hokin-Hikki*, which was written by Tanji Hokin in 1727 and includes many of Musashi's anecdotes, Ben-no-suke used to ask his father many questions about the fighting arts. Sometimes his father couldn't satisfactorily answer the small boy's question, which frustrated him. One day in particular, when Muni-sai was working on something with a small knife, Ben-no-suke came in and started to ask him a question as usual. Muni-sai suddenly lost control of himself and threw the small knife at the young boy in anger. Ben-no-suke easily dodged the knife attack and ran away from his father.

There are two interesting issues suggested by this brief anecdote. One is that Muni-sai's character might not have been a stable one. It is hard to imagine a father would throw a knife at his own child. He could have killed him or, at least, badly injured him. At the same time, it's interesting to ask what it was about Ben-no-suke's attitude that made his father so angry that he risked killing his young son. Muni-sai's unstable personality and Ben-no-suke's precocious behavior are interwoven in this story. Certainly, the lack of a warm, loving relationship between Ben-no-suke and his father would have had a significant influence on the development of Musashi's character.

In the beginning of *The Book of Five Rings*, Musashi writes about engaging in his first combat against the samurai[1] Arima Kihei.[2] Although Ben-no-suke was a mere boy of thirteen, he was exceptional in his physical size and strength. Arima Kihei, a *Shinto-ryu*[3] samurai, did not expect a boy, no matter how big, to be so quick and strong. He was negligent in preparing to meet the unusual challenger. The animal-like Ben-no-suke struck the overconfident samurai to death with a wooden stick. Thus, Musashi's first serious combat took place at the age of thirteen against a real samurai and he was victorious. It remains an impressive event.

His second combat was against a strong samurai named Akiyama,[4] according to Musashi's own words in *The Book of Five Rings*. Musashi was then sixteen years old and was victorious again. When he was seventeen years old he left the village for good. Judging from the fact that there is no record indicating Musashi ever returned, it's safe to assume that he didn't have warm feelings about his home. One can easily imagine that the villagers might not have been particularly kind to him, either. After all, Ben-no-suke killed a man, even though it was the result of a formal combat.

Musashi decided to participate in one of the major civil wars in Japanese history, the Battle of Sekigahara, which took place in A.D. 1600. Unfortunately for Musashi, he joined the wrong side and fought against Ieyasu, who was to become the first shogun of the Tokugawa government, which lasted until 1868. Young Musashi's dream of becoming a high-ranking samurai warrior by distinguishing himself in battle vanished quickly. He started to roam the country as a *ronin* (masterless samurai), developing his abilities and hoping to encounter an opportunity for good employment by a lord. At the age of twenty-one, he went up to Kyoto[5], then the capital, where he engaged in several matches against worthy opponents and won them all. While in Kyoto,[5] Musashi had a chance to challenge a well-known family of martial arts experts, the Yoshiokas,[6] who were in charge of the instruction of martial strategy to Shogun Ashikaga. Musashi decided he had to do something outlandish in order to become well-known, and the battle against the Yoshioka family was his idea of a stepping-stone to fame. It was with a combination of his courage, determination, intelligence, and, of course, fighting skill that he was successful in challenging the Yoshioka family.

Musashi chose the head of the family as his first opponent; if he defeated the head, it was the same as defeating the whole family. The head of the Yoshioka family at that time was Seijuro, and he was no match against Musashi. Seijuro's brother, Denshichiro, attempted to avenge his older brother's defeat, but, he too, was crushed by Musashi. In the end, the whole family, as an army of sorts, challenged Musashi in order to recover their lost face. They made one of Seijuro's young sons, Matashichiro, the symbolic general of the army. They expected Musashi to appear with a small army of warriors to fight the Yoshioka army, but Musashi came alone. According to Musashi, one becomes victor by capturing or killing the general of the enemy. It was unfortunate that this child-general, symbolic or not, had to be used in this way in this particular battle. Musashi's strategy was based on an amoral and pragmatic approach—winning is the most important thing, not how you win. In any event, it is recorded that Musashi killed the young boy during the battle against the large group of Yoshioka samurais, and he declared victory over them.

After this famous battle, Musashi left Kyoto and went to the city of Nara, where he sought out an expert on spear fighting by the name of Ozoin Doei. In facing the spear expert, Musashi theorized that it didn't make much difference whether you held a long sword or a short one against a long weapon such as a spear; in fact, it would make more sense to use a short sword, which could be more easily manipulated once getting into the opponent's fighting range. So, by using a short sword, and with speed and timing, making use of the concept of *sen,* Musashi defeated the spear expert.

It was when Musashi was roaming around the province of Iga (the present Mi-e prefecture) that he heard about Shishido Baiken[7], a master who used a sickle-chain (*kusari-gama*) as his main weapon. The weapon consisted of a sickle and a long chain with a steel ball at the end. Musashi was curious about the unusual weapon and wanted to see how it was used. But the master barred spectators from watching any of the practice sessions. The only way one could see how the sickle-chain was used was to actually engage in combat against the master. People told Musashi that it was a devastating fighting art and no one came close to winning against the master of the sickle-chain.

Musashi decided to challenge Baiken. He entered the small tentlike building where Baiken and his disciples practiced the fighting techniques of their unusual weapon. Baiken accepted Musashi's challenge. As they began the battle, it was a surprise to Baiken as well as to those who witnessed the scene: Musashi stood there with two swords—the longer one in his left hand and the shorter one in his right hand. Baiken must have been confused, for he had never fought anyone holding two swords. He knew if he threw the steel ball that was attached to the end of the chain, Musashi might catch it with one of the swords and counterattack him with the other.

Musashi was aggressive against Baiken, who was forced to retreat. First of all, under normal circumstances, Baiken would have started swinging the steel ball and chain over his head. As he found an opening in his opponent's defense, he would have released the chain and thrown the steel ball against his face. If his opponent happened to catch the ball and chain with his sword, Baiken would have struck his opponent with the sickle and cut his neck. He always had to be on the offense in his posture and movement. But now Baiken was forced to be defensive, fighting against Musashi's two swords. Baiken revealed openings as he went on the defensive. Musashi struck Baiken's chest with the short sword. It did not really hurt him badly but broke his balance as he tried to protect himself against the flying sword. At that moment, Musashi jumped in and, using the long sword, killed the master of the sickle-chain.

Musashi next traveled to Edo (present-day Tokyo), which was then rapidly becoming the center for the commercial as well as political activities of the country. He hoped that he might find a chance for good employment in Edo, but the only openings were in ranks lower than what Musashi expected. It is said that Musashi hoped to attain the rank equivalent to a samurai general who could lead three thousand soldiers in the event of war. Someone employed as an instructor of martial arts by a lord would have been paid from 350 koku to 500 koku per year at most. Koku is a unit of measuring rice used to denote the salary each official received. What Musashi wanted was about ten times that salary. It is clear that Musashi's intention was, if employed by a lord, to do more than just teach the art of sword fighting. He wanted to participate in the decision-making process, to participate in the leadership of the country. As he wrote in *The Book of Five Rings*, Musashi had a deep belief that his fighting strategy was applicable to statesmanship.

In any event, Musashi didn't find suitable employment in Edo. Because of his fame, he could have been hired by any lord without difficulty, but not under the conditions he demanded. While in Edo, Musashi met the samurai Muso Gon-no-suke, the founder of the famous *Shinto-Muso-ryu Jo jitsu*. Gon-no-suke asked Musashi for a match. As Musashi stood against Gon-no-suke, who held a long staff, he might have thought about the time when he faced the spear master in Nara. Musashi held a short stick and, as was his experience against the spear master, his opponent had a long weapon. He still believed, against an opponent with a long weapon, it was more effective to fight holding a short weapon. By using the concept of *sen* most effectively, Musashi got close to Gon-no-suke in such a way that the long staff was no longer useful. Legend has it that Gon-no-suke's encounter with Musashi inspired Gon-no-suke to originate the modern *Jo-do* (the art of the short staff).

Perhaps the most famous combat between two warriors in Japanese history is the one that took place in 1612 between Musashi and another distinguished samurai of the time named Sasaki Kojiro.[8] According to an early book about Musashi, *Niten-ki*,[9] Kojiro was already a retainer of the Hosokawa family as instructor in charge of the art of sword fighting. He was well known for his extraordinary skill with an exceptionally long sword, a style he named *Gan-ryu*. His ability as a sword fighter was unquestionable—he was victorious over every challenger he met. It is said that people feared his long sword as though it possessed a mysterious godlike power.

The fateful meeting between these two extraordinary samurais came about because of several factors. The supporters of the two warriors were curious about how the two compared; Musashi was encouraged by his sponsors to challenge Kojiro for the sake of the pride of some retainers of the Hosokawa family who came from the same family as Musashi; and there was that indefinable something in the egos of these samurai—they could not ignore a challenge. In addition, the pragmatic Musashi would certainly have been lured by the promise of greater fame gained by defeating this famous opponent and thus finally opening a way for

Miyamoto Musashi defeating Sasaki Kojiro on the shore Funa Island (Gan-ryu Island) in the historic duel in 1612. Musashi using two wooden staffs against Kojiro's sword. Woodblock print by Utagawa Kuniyoshi

desirable employment.

This legendary duel lasted for only a few seconds. Musashi used an even longer weapon than Kojiro's well-known long sword. He made a wooden sword out of an old oar. Musashi was so calm and confident that he is said to have made this weapon in a boat on his way to the appointed site of combat. When the two finally met, Kojiro drew his sword first. Musashi dodged it and struck Kojiro's head with his long wooden sword. Musashi's first strike didn't immediately kill Kojiro, who desper-

ately swung his long sword one more time against Musashi as he fell to the ground, but it was in vain. The small island, then called Funa jima, where the dual took place, later was renamed Gan-ryu jima, in memory of Kojiro, the loser, instead of Musashi, the victor.

Regarding the combat between the two outstanding warriors, it was much remarked that Musashi deliberately came late for the encounter; Kojiro had to wait more than two hours for his opponent to arrive. Is this why people later felt more sympathy for Kojiro and renamed the island in Kojiro's memory? Musashi's detractors have used this story to illustrate that there's an aspect of Musashi's strategy which is under-handed and unfair. However, from Musashi's point of view, the important thing was developing a strategy to win, by any means. Losing in combat normally meant death, so one must win at all costs. The combat starts the moment the agreement to meet with swords is made, not at the site of the combat.

Musashi's strategy is based on absolute victory whenever one is engaged in combat. If he thought he would not win, then he would not fight. For Musashi, this was consistent with his strategy of winning at all times. Musashi made Kojiro angry by making him wait for more than two hours at the site of the meet. Anger makes one lose control. Kojiro most likely lost his mental focus, however slightly, and his technique might have become less effective in terms of speed and precision. In other words, Kojiro fell right into the trap of Musashi's strategy.

After the victory over Kojiro, Musashi's name became even more widely known. He could have been hired by any lord, but his demand for an exorbitant salary again prevented that. From Musashi's perspective, he was not just another samurai. There is a distinct difference between Musashi and others as far as interpretation of martial strategy is concerned. Musashi viewed the art of strategy as the highest form of human endeavor, inclusive of all other arts and professions, and others could not comprehend the level of Musashi's strategy, one that transcended mere sword fighting.

Musashi lived most of his life as a *ronin* (masterless samurai). When he was fifty-seven years old, the head of the Hosokawa family, Lord Tadatoshi, invited Musashi as a special guest retainer. Lord Tadatoshi greatly respected and admired Musashi as an outstanding strategist.

Musashi was granted permission for hawking—a privilege reserved for only the highest-ranking samurai of the castle. Although his salary was not high, the prestige was. Musashi might have been satisfied with, and grateful for, Lord Tadatoshi's thoughtful hospitality, and it's likely that through this job Musashi saw a chance to apply his theory and philosophy of strategy to the area of government. Unfortunately, however, this opportunity didn't last long; Lord Tadatoshi died a year after Musashi joined the Hosokawa family.

Musashi's disappointment and pain must have been intense at the loss of his great friend and benefactor, to whom he was ready to dedicate the remainder of his life. However, Musashi's courage and wisdom made him muster his inner power one more time and, for the sake of those who wished to learn his strategy of absolute victory, he sat in a cave called Reigen-do, located close to the Kumamoto[10] castle, and finished *The Book of Five Rings*. It took him a year and eight months. On May 19, 1645, one week after completion of the book, as he meditated in the cave, Musashi passed away at the age of sixty-one.

Shigefumi Kaku

REIGEN-DO
The cave where Musashi spent the last years of his life meditating and where he wrote Gorin no sho (The Book of Five Rings).

MIND OF SAMURAI

BELIEF AND CONFIDENCE:
A MUSASHI ANECDOTE

I t was in the late afternoon of a midsummer day. After traveling all day, Miyamoto Musashi was resting at a small mountain inn, enjoying the scenery as well as a cup of tea. The place was part of Harima province (the present Hyogo[1] prefecture). Musashi's tranquil moment was interrupted when a strange boy approached him. The boy looked very serious. He bowed down deeply to Musashi and started to speak, "Miyamoto *Sensei* (teacher or master). My father was recently killed by a samurai who used a very dishonorable method, and I, as the oldest son of the family, must avenge his death." As he spoke, the boy became even more serious and his voice, trembling, sounded determined to enter a life-or-death combat.

"So, you want me to help you fight your opponent, who killed your father, right?" Musashi asked the boy gently, expecting that the boy should be allowed to have some help in the duel against a samurai. But, surprisingly, the boy shook his head and rejected Musashi's offer, declaring, "I am only thirteen years old and I know I am not strong enough yet to fight a real samurai on an equal basis. But it is my duty to fight him and, if possible, defeat my opponent with my own hands so that my father's soul can rest peacefully in heaven." Musashi was impressed by the boy's proper attitude and strong spirit. It was obvious to Musashi that the boy came from a proud samurai family, for he conducted himself, despite his young age, with a dignity and self-discipline that were becoming of a would-be samurai.

"Miyamoto *Sensei*, I have heard about you from many people. Even my father, while alive, used to speak of you as the greatest warrior in this land." As the boy spoke, his eyes became larger, gradually showing a boyish feature in his manner; he was finally feeling the excitement of meeting the legendary warrior. "Sir, I have one very important request, if I may. Would you please teach me a technique that will make me able to defeat my opponent in this coming duel? I do not fear death, but I want to make sure that I can kill my opponent, no matter what. Is it possible, sir?"

Musashi silently observed the boy's face for a while and, impressed by his earnest attitude as a young samurai, he decided to help him. "All right, young man. Listen to me carefully. I will now give you one very special technique that will make you the victor in the coming duel." Musashi's voice was slow and deliberate. The boy immediately sat down in front of Musashi, in a formal manner, with his eyes intently fixed on Musashi's face.

"Now, this is what you must do. When you meet your opponent, hold the short sword in your left hand and the regular one in your right hand. Carry both swords high above your shoulders as you advance toward your opponent. When the distance between you and your opponent becomes close, stand still and wait for him to attack you first. Your opponent will try to stab you in the chest, at which moment you must quickly parry his attack with your sword in the right hand, and, with all your might, thrust out your short sword in the left hand against your opponent's chest. You must do it as if you are stabbing him through to his back." Musashi stopped here for a few moments and observed the boy with a stern face, but his compassion for the boy was obvious as he continued to talk.

"No matter what happens, don't hesitate to block and attack, for there is no question that you will be victorious. This technique will work for you without doubt." The boy listened to Musashi with total concentration and soon he stood up. He took a short sword in his left hand and the regular sword in the right, as told. It was not easy for the boy to hold the regular sword in one hand, but he tried his best to follow

Musashi's instructions.

"Miyamoto *Sensei*, is this the correct way?" The boy sought Musashi's approval as he wielded the swords repeatedly. The boy was very determined and demonstrated more power and skill than any other thirteen-year-old boy could. "Very good, young man. Very good!" Musashi's heavy voice praised the boy, who was encouraged to continue the same motions many times. After a while, Musashi stopped the boy's practice and said, "Young man, I have one more thing to share with you for your absolute victory in the duel." "Yes, sir." The boy immediately positioned himself in the formal sitting posture and looked anxiously toward Musashi.

"Now, I know that you will be able to avenge your father's death, without doubt, by using the technique that I have just taught you." Musashi stressed the boy's would-be victory, after which he became silent. He slowly moved his eyes to the sky, which was getting dark, but still one could see a brilliant red color over the mountains far away. Was it that Musashi was reminiscing about his first duel when he killed Arima Kihei? Musashi, then called Ben-no-suke, had been thirteen years old at that time, the same age as the boy.

Musashi looked down at the boy again and, in a mysterious tone, started to speak. "There is no question that you are going to win in this battle. But you are still young and your opponent is an experienced samurai. I think it is good if I give you an additional power that will make you certain of your victory. That is, I am going to pray to the God of Ants, who will protect you against your opponent for sure. As you stand facing your opponent, just before you advance toward him, remember to look down at the ground where you stand. If an ant is found crawling around near your feet, it means that the God of Ants has listened to my prayer and in no way can you lose." So saying, Musashi closed his eyes and started to pray, pressing his palms together. The boy watched Musashi and followed the gesture of praying.

It is important to note that Musashi directly mentions in one of his writings, *Dokko-Do* (*The Path of Lone Walk*), "I respect Buddha and gods, but I do not depend on them," which highlights Musashi's absolute belief in self-power, *ji-riki*. Therefore, whatever he was doing for the sake of the boy's situation, Musashi's gesture of praying to the

God of Ants was not religious in nature. Rather, it was a gesture to induce a certain psychological strength in the young samurai.

In any event, on the day of the duel, the boy dressed in a colorful costume with a white headband—his father would have been very proud of him. As he walked to the site of the duel, the boy's face was full of concentration and determination. He saw his opponent in the distance. The boy stopped to draw the two swords, as instructed by Musashi. He raised both swords high above his shoulders and was then ready to advance toward the opponent. He then remembered to look down at the ground where he stood, hoping to find an ant as the sure sign of his victory, as Musashi had told him. It was in the middle of summer. You couldn't miss an ant on the ground, no matter where you looked. Not only one or two, but hundreds of small ants were crawling all around his feet. The boy became even more confident of his victory, believing that the God of Ants was on his side, as Musashi had prayed on his behalf.

The boy walked toward his opponent with a confident manner and with his eyes focused on the opponent at all times. As predicted by Musashi, the opponent thrust out the sword to stab the boy in the chest. The boy blocked it with the sword in his right hand and counter-attacked with the short sword in his left hand. The boy won, successfully avenging his father's death and thus restoring honor to his family.

As this anecdote indicates, Musashi's greatness lies not only in the fact that he was an extraordinary fighting strategist, but also that he was a psychologist of sorts. Musashi used a psychological technique to get the boy to believe in himself and absolute victory, which resulted in the defeat of a samurai by a mere thirteen-year-old boy. If we ignore the social background in which Musashi had to survive, it is easy to be misled into thinking of him as a ruthless, cunning character. But, as we can appreciate from this story, he was compassionate as well. His intelligence was also noteworthy, especially for a samurai of that era. It is now known that psychology, properly administered, is a powerful tool in accomplishing many things. Musashi was already familiar with this mental strategy in his time and used it to induce an almost miraculous inner strength in the boy by "psyching him up." Musashi himself must have used the same technique to encourage himself and to survive more than sixty combats, all of which he won.

VICTORY WITHOUT FIGHTING:
A BOKUDEN ANECDOTE

Tsukahara Bokuden,[2] one of the best-known warriors of sixteenth-century Japan, used to travel with many followers. On one occasion he was traveling alone by boat. Although it was obvious that he was a samurai because of the two swords he carried, no one recognized that he was the legendary warrior. On the boat, there were many people from all walks of life, including merchants, craftsmen, farmers, and a few samurais.

There was one particular samurai on the same boat who was talking loudly and drawing a great deal of attention to himself. He was busy bragging about his ability with the sword, claiming he was one of the best sword fighters in the country. People were afraid of him, so they pretended to show an interest in his story. But one person, who was sitting alone away from the others, did not seem to be interested in the samurai's story at all. It was Bokuden, who was minding his own business.

The samurai walked over to Bokuden and demanded attention from him. But Bokuden continued to ignore him, which really irritated the samurai. At last, the samurai became so angry that he challenged Bokuden to a duel. But Bokuden refused to engage in sword fighting in such a crowded place, as innocent people could get hurt. The samurai agreed to wait until the boat reached the nearest shore, and he ordered the boatman to direct the boat to the nearest island.

While waiting for the boat to arrive at the island, the samurai was already very excited, and he swung his sword in front of people many times to loosen up for the combat. Bokuden was lying down, resting with his eyes closed. Finally, when the boat came very close to the island, the bragging samurai shouted, "Come! You are now as good as dead. I will show you how sharp my sword is!" Bokuden did not reply but got up slowly. The samurai jumped off the boat and landed on the shore with the sword in his hands. As soon as the samurai stepped on the shore, Bokuden took the oar from the boatman and pushed the boat away from the shore. "You coward bastard!" the samurai screamed loudly, swinging his sword. But Bokuden was calm and laughing as he declared, "This is what is called Victory Without Fighting." People in the boat laughed, watching the screaming samurai on the land, and at the same time, they were all impressed by Bokuden's tactics. Once they learned who Bokuden was, people bowed down to him with reverence.

When you consider Bokuden's attitude in dealing with the bragging, pugnacious samurai, you may be struck by his calmness, which was the result of confidence in his own ability. A truly confident person never loses self-control in whatever situation he is forced into. Bokuden was not the least disturbed by the samurai's challenge to a duel, which would have been a life-and-death combat. In contrast to Bokuden's serene, mature manner, which is that of a truly strong person, the arrogant samurai's attitude was almost comical. In any society, there are always insecure individuals who boast about whatever they think they are, or whatever they think they can do. This type of individual is usually desperately seeking recognition and attention from others. Of course, it is natural that one wants to be "counted" and to be thought of as someone of worth. But it is comical when an individual demonstrates this desire, basic to all human beings, in an antisocial, undisciplined, and immature way.

It should also be appreciated that Bokuden, who was believed to be virtually invincible in sword fighting, did not respond to the bad samurai's challenge in the manner that an ordinary person might have expected. It would have been very easy for him to face this threatening samurai with his sword and cut him down with one stroke. But Bokuden was not eager to use his awesome skill in sword fighting. Again, the truism exists in any society—a really strong person does not resort to violence unless it is absolutely unavoidable. Bokuden knew that life is precious, no matter what, and at the same time, he knew he had to teach a lesson to the belligerent samurai. Bokuden considered his skill of sword fighting to be too precious to be used against a samurai of such low attitude. The superiority of the true master was obvious in his non-aggressive attitude.

It is also noteworthy that Bokuden's ingenuity taught the bad samurai a lesson in a more devastating way than fighting could have done. If killed, the samurai would have never learned a lesson. If he was injured in combat against Bokuden, it would only have shown that he was defeated in combat by Bokuden. But when he was left alone on the shore, shouting helplessly, he realized that his mind was no match against Bokuden's. This was a great lesson to him as well as to those who watched the scene. Considering the fact that losing face is the worst humiliation for a samurai, Bokuden's tactics defeated the man more clearly than any other way.

It brings to mind the story of a brutish man who wanted to destroy a bicycle by smashing it on the ground. After throwing the bicycle against the ground several times, it was still functional. Another man came by. He was a master of martial arts and asked what the man was doing. The brutish man replied, "I want to destroy this bicycle and get a new one. So I'm smashing it against the ground." The martial arts master quietly bent down and, with his two fingers, took the chain off the bicycle and said to the brute man, "I think your bicycle is dead now." In observing the world situation, one cannot help wondering why there are so many military conflicts, large and small, that always bring hardship, misery, and pain to ordinary citizens. There must be methods of resolution other than ones that involve the use of weapons of destruction, no matter how complicated and difficult the problems may be.

A RESOLUTE MIND:
A MASAHIRO ANECDOTE

There was a distinguished samurai by the name of Adachi Masahiro who lived in the latter part of the eighteenth century. He was apparently familiar with the power of mind properly applied to sword fighting. Of course, physical technique in sword fighting is important, and that is why a samurai had to go through incredible physical training in order to attain proficiency in physical skills of fighting. But, as a great swordsman, Adachi Masahiro aptly observed that a warrior with superb physical skill would not be as effective as an opponent of lesser technical skill but greater mental strength based on determination, courage, and willpower. It is true that too often we have a tendency to underestimate the power of the mind, looking for an answer in something more tangible and more easily explainable. The following story was told by Adachi Masahiro to his disciples to illustrate the point.

A servant who worked for a certain lord committed a very serious mistake by offending a high-ranking samurai of another clan. Of course, it was an accident, but it was demanded that the servant be put to death to satisfy the offended samurai. The lord, whose political position was not high, and thus did not have much influence over the decision of the other clan, could not bear the thought of surrendering the servant to be killed. But something had to be done to offer a sincere apology to the samurai and to the clan to which he belonged. After much contemplation on the matter, the lord requested that his servant be given a chance to engage in a contest of sword fighting. Of course, being a servant, he had never had a chance to train in sword fighting. The agreement was made that the servant was allowed to participate in the contest and if, by any chance, he won the contest, he would be pardoned.

It was a very special arrangement, for, under normal circumstances, it was impossible for a servant to be able to participate in a contest of samurai sword fighting. Needless to say, no one expected to see the servant survive in the contest against warriors of great skill and experience. The lord told the servant, "I cannot bear the thought of surrendering you to their hand to be killed as the punishment for your mistake. Now it seems that the only way we can save your life is for you to come out of this contest of sword fighting as the winner. It is stipulated that you will be pardoned if you win the contest. I am sorry that this is the best that I have been able to do for you." The servant replied with tears in his eyes to the compassionate lord, "Master, you have been much too kind to me, such a lowly individual. I am eternally grateful for your kindness in trying to save my life. But, Master, as you are fully aware, I am just a servant and I know only the most basic technique of sword fighting and am no way capable of competing against those samurais whose profession is to train themselves in martial arts, especially the art of sword fighting. I am as good as dead either way. I would have no chance against those warriors if I fight, and if I don't fight, they will kill me anyway." The servant showed a face of complete relinquishment. The lord asked the servant with slow and clear voice, "Are you truly sure that you are ready to die?" "Yes, Master. I am ready to die at any moment." At this answer, the lord smiled and told the servant that despite all odds the servant would not lose in the contest if he maintained the same mental attitude of facing death without fear.

On the day of the contest, the onlookers were amazed to see the servant's most unexpected strength in sword fighting. His opponents all froze when they saw the servant's eyes. The servant slowly came close to each opponent and struck his head with precision. The contest came to the final match, between the servant and the samurai whom he had accidentally offended. The samurai demanded that the match be fought with real swords. The permission was granted for the match with real swords, which meant it was going to be a life-and-death combat. All matches until then had been conducted with bamboo swords lest the participants get hurt unnecessarily. Now tension was high with the likelihood that one of combatants would die. The samurai knelt and prayed before the match, but the servant's attitude was the same as it had been, calm and stoic.

The match did not last long. The samurai, completely overwhelmed by the determined servant, gave up in the middle of the contest, for fear that he would not be able to defeat the servant. A noted warrior with distinction in sword fighting, the samurai could not understand the whole thing: how this man of low class without much knowledge in sword fighting could overcome him. Adachi Masahiro explained to his disciples that the difference was the servant's mind—one that was based on a complete lack of fear of death—which enabled him not to worry about the outcome of the contest. He let his mind move freely and the sword moved according to the perfectly free mind, being detached from all worldly thoughts. No one could defeat a man in that mental condition, for it transcended ordinary technical skill and strength.

If a person is determined to accomplish something without fear of the outcome, nothing is impossible. When you face a seemingly impossible problem, an opponent of twice your strength, or a huge responsibility that makes you tremble, you must remember the story of this humble servant who outshone all samurai warriors in their game at the most critical moment. One starts truly living when one relinquishes attachment to things as they are. True power is produced when one's conscious power is released from within the self.

PART II
THE BOOK
OF FIVE RINGS

VOLUME ONE **EARTH**

TRANSLATION

Herein, I intend to describe my martial strategy for the first time. My fighting style is called *Niten-Ichi-ryu*, and I have trained myself in it for many years. It is now the early part of October in the twentieth year of the Kan ei Era.[1] I climbed the Iwato mountain, which is located in Higo[2] of Kyusyu[3] Island. I then prayed to heaven, knelt in front of Kan-non,[4] and paid proper respects to Buddha.

I am a samurai[5] by the name of Musashi no Kami Fujiwara no Genshin, born in the Harima[6] prefecture, and am now sixty years old.

Ever since my youth, I have always been interested in and studied the way of martial strategy. I engaged in my first actual combat when I was thirteen years old. My opponent at that time was a samurai of Shinto-ryu[7] style by the name of Arima Kihei, whom I defeated. At the age of sixteen, I was triumphant over a strong and capable samurai named Akiyama from the province of Tajima. At twenty-one, I went up to Kyoto[8] City and encountered martial strategists of all kinds from throughout the country; I fought some of them and never even lost once.

After my experience in Kyoto, I roamed the country and encountered strategists of different styles. I engaged in a total of over sixty combats and won all of them. This took place between the ages of thirteen and twenty-eight or twenty-nine.

However, after the age of thirty, I started to reflect on my experiences and began to wonder whether or not my victories were attributable to my natural ability, sheer luck, or the inferior techniques of those whom I had defeated, rather than my true understanding of the principle of martial strategy. Since that realization, I started to train myself particularly hard in order to attain the profound doctrine of martial strategy. Finally, when I reached fifty years of age, I found myself in complete harmony with the principle of martial strategy.

Once I became enlightened by the true meaning of martial strategy, I ceased to have any real interest or desire in the worldly affairs. As a result of my application of the principle of martial strategy to my daily living, I found that I had no need for a teacher or special instructor, no matter what arts or professions I attempted to engage in.

As I sit down here to begin writing this book, I do not intend to use any archaic words from the scriptures of Buddhism or Confucianism, nor will I depend on the examples of various writings of old war chronicles and battle tactics. With a sincere heart, I will now begin to explain *Niten-Ichi-ryu* as it is reflected in the Way of Heaven and Kan-non. It is now 4:00 A.M. on the tenth day of October, 1643.

Martial strategy is the foundation of the samurai family. The head of the family should train particularly hard in the art of strategy, but the soldiers must also acquaint themselves with it. Nowadays, I regret to say that we do not find a samurai with a true understanding of martial strategy.

In this world we live in, there exist various disciplines to protect and further people's wellbeing. For example, Buddhism is the Way of salvation; Confucianism the Way of learning. A physician engages in the Way of healing people's illnesses, while a poet teaches the Way of poems.

There are also those who specialize in the tea ceremony and the Way of archery, and so on. Generally speaking, people who are involved in these arts and professions seem to be enthusiastic about their Ways, expressing their belief and enjoyment in each field. However, it is rare to find a person who enjoys the Way of martial strategy.

In any case, a samurai must engage in two forms of discipline as a rule, the literary and the military. In accordance with his duty and position, a samurai must constantly train in this Way regardless of whether he is particularly able.

It is often said that a samurai must be prepared to die at any time.

But if dying is important, anyone can do it: there is no difference in the deaths of a priest, a woman, a peasant, and other classes of people who would die for the sake of obligation and personal shame. What makes a samurai different is that he has to try to defeat the opponent(s) at any cost. In other words, a samurai may defeat his opponent in one-to-one combat or he may be single-handedly victorious over several opponents. He does this for the sake of his lord, whom he serves, and for his own pride and honor. All these things are only possible if a samurai faithfully follows the Way of martial strategy.

There may be those who doubt the usefulness of martial strategy in actual combat situations. But it is important that one should constantly train in martial strategy so that it can become effective and useful in every aspect of life and at any point in time. One who teaches the Way of martial strategy must also follow the true Way, presenting it in such a way that it can be useful at any time.

CONCERNING THE WAY OF MARTIAL STRATEGY

In China as well as in Japan, those who practice this Way have been called "experts" of martial strategy. It is essential that a samurai should study this Way.

Nowadays, we hear about people who call themselves "strategists," but they only deal with the techniques of sword fighting. Priests from such shrines as Kashima and Katori[9] in the province of Hitachi[10] prefecture have recently started to teach strategies by claiming that the gods have handed down the techniques to them. From olden times, people have always spoken of ten talents and seven arts, of which martial strategy is one. It is true that martial strategy brings a certain benefit, but in order to make the most of it one must not limit oneself to the study of sword fighting alone. This is too limited to be called martial strategy.

Throughout society there are people who can be seen using their arts as objects to sell. Various tools are also often made just to be sold, which is akin to having a tree with more flowers than fruit. Particularly in the field of martial strategy there are those who use colorful gestures in order to attract people's attention and show off their techniques. They often manage more than one dojo[11] and teach martial strategy to make a profit. Both those who teach as well as those who learn in this fashion should reflect on what they are doing. It has been said, "Martial strategy without true substance is often the cause of grave wounds to its practitioners," which is, indeed, correct.

Generally speaking, people in society can be categorized in four classes: samurais, farmers, artisans, and merchants. One of them, farmers, must prepare various tools so that they can respond to the change of seasons. They must always live well prepared. This is the Way of the farmers.

Secondly, there is the Way of the merchants. For example, some produce *sake*[12] by acquiring the necessary ingredients and by utilizing certain tools so that they can make the proper profits. The Way of the merchants is based on the idea that each person makes the profit that he deserves according to his ability and effort.

The third Way is that of the samurai, who must understand, among other things, that he must make his own weapons. He must become familiar with the usage of each weapon as well. Without knowledge of weapons and their proper usage, one cannot call oneself a true samurai.

The fourth Way is that of the artisans. A carpenter's Way is to devise various tools and learn how to use them well. Furthermore, he must work with a square in order to have correct plans to work from. He regards time as valuable and does not take off from work too often. These are the Ways of a farmer, a merchant, a samurai, and an artisan.

Now, let me explain to you martial strategy in terms of the carpenter's Way. The reason for making such a comparison is that both concepts can be equated with the idea of a house. A noble house ("clan"), a samurai house, the Fujiwara clan's four houses,[13] destruction or continuous existence of a certain house, a certain style, a certain trend, and a certain house's tradition can all be compared to the concept of martial strategy. Therefore, I will now attempt to explain martial strategy using the example of the Way of the carpenter who builds houses.

The word "carpenter" is expressed in two Chinese characters, "major" and "device." Thus, the Way of martial strategy should also be seen as a major device. If one wishes to learn martial strategy, one's full attention must be focused on reading this book. The person who teaches and the person who learns should share a relationship of mutual respect and congeniality like a needle and thread. They should be constantly training.

THE METAPHOR OF MARTIAL STRATEGY AND THE CARPENTER

A general should familiarize himself with the overall condition of the nation and correctly assess it in the same manner as a head carpenter would familiarize himself with the scale of a house. The head carpenter should know the makeup of towers and temples as well as the design of palaces. He directs others to build houses and buildings; the same thing can be said of the head of a samurai house.

In order to build a house one must be able to discern different types of wood[14]. A straight wood without knots, which has a beautiful appearance, should be used for the front pillars, while a strong, straight wood with some knots should be used for the rear pillars. A beautiful-looking wood without knots but which happens to be weak should be used to make thresholds, lintels, and sliding doors. A strong wood, even if knotted and warped to some degree, can be used for the strong foundation of the house, where it is not too visible. In other words, use each material appropriately, according to its characteristics, so that the house may last a long time. As for a weak wood which is warped and has a lot of knots, you should consider using such wood as scaffolding and later as firewood.

Likewise, in order to do the job as efficiently as possible, the head carpenter should discern each worker's ability and use each of them in different positions according to their talent, or lack of it. The carpenters can be set to work on the sliding doors, thresholds, lintels, and ceiling, depending on their capability and experience. Someone without experience or ability should be given the job of flooring, while the worst one should just make wedges. In this way you do not have to waste manpower.

The head carpenter should keep the following things in mind at all times:

- One must be efficient and perform the jobs well.
- One should not take things too lightly.
- One must keep a sense of the priorities in mind.
- One must be sensitive to other people's moods.
- One should be able to recognize that which is not possible.

These things are also directly applicable to the principle of martial strategy.

THE WAY OF MARTIAL STRATEGY

A soldier can be compared to a carpenter who makes and polishes all the tools which he carries in his work box. The carpenter must listen carefully to the head carpenter's orders. He has to plan the pillars and polish the floor; he also has to be able to engage in some sculpturing. He should also measure all parts of the building correctly and do each task well no matter how difficult it may be. This is the Way of the carpenter. With increased skill and experience in his craft, he will eventually become a head carpenter.

A carpenter must remember always to be equipped with sharp and useful tools, which he must sharpen whenever he can. By utilizing these tools, an expert carpenter should be able to make a variety of things, from a miniature shrine to bookshelves, a table, a paper lantern, a cuttingboard, and even pot lids. A soldier's duty is akin to that of a carpenter. This point must be reflected upon and understood well.

A carpenter pays careful attention to his projects to ensure that they are not warped, that the joints are properly connected, that they are well-planed, not just sanded for the sake of a smooth appearance alone. A carpenter must also make sure that the finished products do not warp later on. If you want to learn and improve yourself in the Way of martial strategy, you must pay close attention to each of the things written in this book.

THE DIVISION OF THIS
BOOK INTO FIVE PARTS

I have divided the Way of martial strategy into five parts, each of which explains a certain important theory. The five divisions are the volumes *Earth, Water, Fire, Wind* and *Kū*.[15]

In the volume *Earth*, I describe the general principles of the Way of martial strategy and explain the fundamental view regarding my style. It is difficult to attain the high stage of the Way if your study is limited purely to the art of sword fighting. It is vital that one should be able to grasp a small concept from observing a larger one; similarly, one must learn how to reach a deeper area from a more shallow one. This section has been named *Earth* because it represents the preparation, the groundwork, for a road that will lead you to the straight path.

The second section is the volume *Water*, in which I try to show you how to make your mind become like water. Water adjusts itself to any kind of container; it can become one drop and at the same time it can become an ocean. I shall use the basic nature of water—blue and clear—to explain matters concerning my style.

By mastering the underlying principles of sword fighting, you can as easily defeat your opponent as anyone else in the world. The essence of victory is the same whether it be over one or ten thousand opponents.

A general's martial strategy must be such that he is able to visualize something large from a small model, like building a large statue of Buddha from a miniature sample. It is a difficult concept to explain in writing, but, in short, the principle of martial strategy is based on the idea of understanding many things from one small thing. Matters concerning my style are described in this volume called *Water*.

The third section is the volume *Fire*, in which I write about matters relating to actual battles. Fire can be either furious or calm, which is the reason why it is an appropriate metaphor for actual battles. The principle of combat is the same whether it concerns one-to-one combat situations or warfare involving armies. You must try to understand it through the mental exercise of grasping an overall situation as well as dealing with the details.

It is easy to see something large, while it takes an effort to observe something small. In other words, in a large group situation movement is slow and not easily manageable. But a single person's mind can change so quickly and inconspicuously that it is difficult to follow it. This point must be examined carefully.

The volume *Fire* addresses times of emergency. One must constantly train one's mind so that in emergency situations one has an ordinary, calm state of mind. This is the reason why I write about actual combats in this volume.

The fourth section is the volume *Wind*. I do not deal with the matters concerning my style in this volume, but I write here about the various different martial strategies and philosophies which we see nowadays in society in general; "wind" refers to fashion such as "old fashion," "present fashion," and "each family's fashion." Thus, I write about the different "fashions" of present martial strategies in society as a whole and the techniques of each style, and call it *Wind*.

Without knowing other matters and people, one cannot know oneself well. In many arts or situations one could function without knowing that his method is not a right one from the viewpoint of the true Way. An erroneous Way can be the result of a slight lack of concentration which will make one stray from the true Way. If one does not follow the strict doctrine of the true Way, even a small deviation can result in a serious fault in the long run. This point must be examined well.

It is not surprising to me that in other styles it is believed that martial strategy consists purely of sword-fighting techniques. Martial strategy is based on a particular meaning. In order to inform my readers of present-day martial strategies, I have decided to write about matters concerning other styles in this volume *Wind*.

The fifth volume is called *Kū*.[16] Since it is called *Kū* there is neither depth nor beginning. Having reached the highest principle of my martial strategy, one then goes beyond it by detaching oneself from the principle; furthermore, one gains control of the martial strategy by harmonizing oneself with it. Without conscious effort one finds oneself master of the rhythm of each combat situation and becomes able to strike the opponent at any time. This is the Way of *Kū*. I will write about the matter of pursuing the true Way in this volume.

NAMING THIS STYLE *NITO*

Whether a general or a foot soldier, a samurai must always carry two swords. In olden times, they used to call them *tachi* (long sword) and *katana* (sword), and nowadays, *katana* (sword) and wakizashi (short sword or auxilary sword). A samurai, without any question, should carry these two swords, which is in accordance with the proper custom. Whether one is truly conscious of it or not, the two swords represent the Way of samurai. In order to explain the reasoning behind the two swords, I call my style *Niten-Ichi-ryu* ("Two-Heaven-One style"). A spear and a halberd are normally not considered the samurai's primary tools, but they are still part of a samurai's weapons. In my style we make a beginner practice holding a sword in one hand and a short sword in the other hand at the same time. In a life-or-death situation, it would make sense to use every weapon at one's disposal. It would not be sensible for one to die without having taken advantage of all available weapons.

However, when one holds a sword in each hand simultaneously, it becomes difficult to manipulate them both effectively. Hence the reason for practicing with the two swords at the same time: to enable one to handle a sword with one hand easily. The larger weapons such as the spear and halberd have to be manipulated with two hands, while a sword and short sword can be handled with one hand only. It is not practical to hold a sword with both hands while on horseback, while running, or while engaging in a battle in a swamp, in a deep rice field, in a field full of stones, on a steep road, or in a place crowded with people. While holding a bow, a spear, and other weapons in the left hand, one can still handle a sword in the other. It is not correct to hold a sword with both hands as one faces an opponent. If it becomes difficult to kill the opponent with one hand then one should use both hands to swing the sword more effectively. It is not a particularly difficult matter to practice with a sword in each hand, the main purpose of which is to learn how to wield a sword effectively with one hand.

It is natural that everyone should experience some difficulty in managing a sword with one hand in the beginning as it feels very heavy. But this is true of other things; they are all difficult to handle in the beginning. For example, pulling a bowstring or swinging a halberd is not easy in the beginning. But as one trains, it becomes easier to draw the bow. With constant training in the Way of sword fighting, by attaining its principle, it becomes easier to wield a sword. The essence of the techniques of the sword-fighting art does not lie in speed, which I shall explain in the volume *Water*. The fundamental principle of the sword-fighting art is that one should utilize a longer sword in a wide space and take advantage of a short sword in a narrow area.

A tenet of my teaching is that one must win regardless of the length of the sword one uses, so I do not dictate the length of the sword. The ultimate objective of my style is to be prepared to win, no matter what weapons are involved. It is more advantageous to hold two swords, one in each hand, when you have to fight multiple opponents alone or when you are surrounded by many opponents. These things should be clear to you by now without further explanation. Through understanding one thing you must be able to grasp things that are not explicit. By attaining the high stage of martial strategy, you will come to understand whatever needs to be understood. Try to appreciate and study this well.

UNDERSTANDING THE
TWO CHARACTERS *"HYO-HO"*

In the field of martial strategy (*"hyo-ho"*) in general, it is customary to call someone who can handle a sword well a "martial strategist." In the martial arts, someone who is adept in the art of the bow is called an archer; someone who knows how to handle a gun well is called a marksman; someone who is proficient in the use of the spear is called a spear user; and someone who has mastered the techniques of a halberd is called a halberd user. Following this custom, we should call someone who has attained a high level of proficiency in the techniques of sword fighting a swordsman. It also follows that someone who knows how to use a short sword superbly should be called a short-sword user. A bow, a gun, a spear, and a halberd are all the instruments of the samurai family, therefore, they are part of the Way of martial strategy. As far as a sword is concerned, its user is not called a swordsman; instead, he is called a martial strategist. There is a good reason for this.

The foundation of martial strategy is the Way of the sword, for one learns how to govern people and how to discipline oneself through the Way of the sword. By mastering the principles of sword fighting, one can be victorious over ten opponents. Similarly, by utilizing the same principles, one hundred men should be able to defeat ten thousand opponents. Therefore, according to my martial strategy, the number of fighters involved does not matter in the basic principle of the strategy. Thus, all the doctrines and principles concerning the samurai's methods are included in martial strategy.

Normally the Way of the samurai does not include the Ways of a Confucianist, a Buddhist, a tea practitioner, an etiquette specialist, or a dancer. But if one truly pursues a Way, no matter in what field of endeavor, he will eventually come to share a common ground of truth with other people who have become highly accomplished in different fields. It is important that each person train with diligence and sincerity in the field of their choice.

UNDERSTANDING THE PROPER USAGE OF WEAPONS

Understanding how to use each weapon correctly is crucial, as one must apply each weapon in the appropriate time and situation. For example, a short sword is useful when engaging in battle in a limited space or when you and your opponent are fighting close together in hand-to-hand combat. A regular sword is useful almost anywhere and so it is very valuable. On the battlefield, a halberd may not be as effective as a spear, because the former is a defensive weapon while the latter is offensive. If two warriors are of equivalent fighting skill, the one with a spear has a slight advantage. A spear and a halberd are only useful in certain situations and they are not too convenient in limited spaces. Neither are they particularly effective when you are surrounded by opponents. It is primarily as battlefield instruments that they can be useful.

Trying to learn how to use weapons inside a house, emphasizing minor aspects and ignoring the real application, will be of no use. On the battlefield, a bow can be useful in executing various tactics: for example, it can be particularly effective in shooting arrows rapidly from spaces in between the spearmen and others with weapons. It is of little use in the siege of castles or when the enemy is positioned at a distance of more than forty yards.

Nowadays, in the martial arts, there are too many decorative elements which clearly lack substance (the bow included)—they will not be of any use in emergency situations. Probably the most useful weapon is a firearm, especially when attacking opponents from inside a castle. Even on the battlefield, a firearm is very effective before the actual hand-to-hand combat begins. However, once actual combat starts a firearm is not very useful. One of the advantages of the bow is that one can follow the path of an arrow as it is shot, while it is not possible to follow the bullets of a firearm with one's eyes. This is an important point and must be studied carefully.

As for a horse, endurance and lack of peculiar habits are important considerations. Generally speaking, one must ensure that one's weapons are well built and of a good size. In other words, a horse should be large and strong; a sword should be sufficiently large and sharp. A spear and a halberd should be of good size as well and should be able to penetrate well; a bow and a gun should be chosen for their sturdiness. One should not show any favoritism toward one weapon over the others; the same thing can be said regarding other things in life. Excessiveness is just as bad as its opposite. You must choose your weapon wisely so that it fits your own characteristics, not imitate others. Both generals and soldiers should avoid being particular about things. It is important to consider this well.

"HYOSHI"[17] IN MARTIAL STRATEGY

There is something called *hyoshi* ("rhythm-timing") in everything in life, but the "rhythm-timing" in martial strategy is something special and cannot be acquired without diligent training.

In society in general, dancing and music most clearly demonstrate the notion of rhythm-timing. Their performances demonstrate a certain harmony of rhythm-timing. In the field of martial arts, one finds rhythm-timing in the techniques of shooting an arrow, firing a gun and riding a horse. The concept of rhythm-timing should not be ignored in any profession or art.

There is a certain rhythm-timing in intangible matters as well. For example, there is rhythm-timing in prosperity with which one can be successful in one's duty to one's lord; at the same time, one can fail in serving the lord through bad rhythm-timing. There is rhythm-timing in harmony as well as in discord. In the business world, for example, there is rhythm-timing with which a merchant becomes rich or a rich person becomes poor. There are different rhythm-timings in different fields. It is important to be able to judge and appreciate the rhythm-timing of things in general and see whether a particular rhythm timing is in harmony with prosperity or will lead to your decline.

There are also various rhythm-timings in martial strategy as well. First of all, one should perceive the most effective and advantageous rhythm-timing and differentiate it from other negative rhythm-timings. One should be able to use well-chosen rhythm-timings out of various rhythm-timings. It is important to learn how to solve a problem of distance by using a particular rhythm-timing. One should also realize that rhythm-timing can work to turn a situation to one's advantage. This is crucial in martial strategy.

In combat, you must first perceive your opponent's rhythm-timing and then execute your techniques with a rhythm-timing that your opponent would never expect. This unexpected rhythm-timing is the result of your constant training that becomes spontaneous. I will discuss this matter of rhythm-timing in every volume to make sure that you understand it well. Study it well.

I have thus far described the *Niten-Ichi-ryu* Way of martial strategy which can only be learned through vigorous training. Once the training is acquired, its practitioner will be naturally enlightened as to the true meaning of martial strategy, which is applicable to one-to-one combat as well as warfare involving armies. This is the first time that I have written about my martial strategy for the sake of others in the volumes *Earth, Water, Fire, Wind,* and *Kū*.

Those who wish to study my martial strategy should abide by the following teachings:[18]

- One should embrace thoughts that are morally correct.

- One should diligently train at all times.
- One should become familiar with various arts.
- One should acquire knowledge of other professions.
- One should be aware in general of gain and loss.
- One should cultivate the ability to appreciate and judge things correctly.
- One should try to perceive things that are not apparent to the human eye.
- One should pay attention to even the most seemingly insignificant matters.
- One should avoid engaging in unproductive matters.

In the pursuit of martial strategy your training should comply with the above tenets. Without a broad vision of perceiving the truth clearly one cannot become a true expert in the world of martial strategy. Once you master my martial strategy you will be able to defeat twenty or thirty opponents by yourself. It is essential that you always maintain the spirit of martial strategy, training constantly in pursuit of the Way. You will become capable of defeating your opponent(s) through physical techniques as well as by the power of insight. You will also be able to overcome your opponent(s) with your physical prowess and mental strength, which will be the result of your training and discipline in the Way of my martial strategy. Once you attain this level of proficiency in my strategy, how can anyone defeat you in combat?

When applying martial strategy to the world of leadership, it is important that you make the acquaintance of people of good character; that you become a good leader to others; that you conduct yourself in a correct manner; that you govern people well; that you take good care of others; that you follow and maintain the laws and customs of the land for the sake of order; and that you never take second place to anyone in whatever you engage. In this way you will become prosperous in your position and gain personal honor and success. This is in accordance with the true Way of martial strategy.

To: Terao Magonojo

May 12, 1645
Shin-men Musashi

ANALYSIS

I n the accomplishment of any task in any field, one's determination, based on self-discipline and willpower, is the most important thing. This serious attitude can be expressed in different ways according to the person involved. One may spend some time in meditation before embarking on an actual task. Another person may choose a special place where he or she is about to spend a considerable amount of time in accomplishing a work, whether it be a painting, writing, or study.

Musashi's serious intention concerning this book is well expressed as he declares that he begins writing the book at 4:00 A.M. on October 10, 1643, in the cave called Reigen-do, located on the outskirts of the province of Higo (presently the Kumamoto prefecture). It is further mentioned that he prayed to heaven and paid his proper respects to the images of Buddha and the goddess of mercy, by which action Musashi might have demonstrated a sacred and selfless motivation for writing the book.

It is interesting to note that Musashi says that he respects Buddha and the gods but that he does not depend on them. His absolute confidence and belief in himself as the source of strength was kept alive to the end of his life. Nevertheless, Musashi humbly recognizes that there is an unknown element in the world, something beyond human understanding. He does not ignore the existence of Buddha's spirit and the gods as the sacred source of guidance for ordinary human affairs. He believes, however, that he does not need help from them. No matter how great a person is, he or she cannot escape the most fundamental condition of being human. Musashi expresses his absolute certainty in human potential while at the same time admitting his own limitations as a finite being. Einstein said the more he explored the universe, the greater the sense of humility he felt about his own finiteness.[19]

The implication of the time when Musashi starts to write the book, should also be noted. As he states, it was at 4:00 A.M. Generally speaking, we experience certain benefits when we begin a task in early morning, rather than in the afternoon or evening. There is something special and precious about the morning air, a positive feeling. According to some leading Japanese executives of major companies, it is generally agreed that important negotiations and meetings are more likely to succeed if they take place in the morning rather than in the afternoon or evening. (Needless to say, however, some people function more effectively in a variety of different work capacities in the afternoon or evening.)

The most noteworthy of Musashi's introductory remarks concerns his personal history. The autobiographical notes are brief but are the only reliable source of information on Musashi's life. Thus, their importance from a historical viewpoint cannot be overstated.

There is a book called *Niten-ki* ("The Chronicle of Two Heavens"),[20] which was written about one hundred years after Musashi's death. The book contains Musashi's biography but, unfortunately, the historical "facts" are not very reliable—there is a lot of exaggeration and distortion. Perhaps the writers' adoration and respect for Musashi obscured their sense of historical accuracy. There is another important book concerning Musashi's life called *Tanji-Hokin-Hikki* ("The Transcript by Tanji Hokin"). It was written in 1727, just about the same time as *Niten-ki*, but again, its historical accuracy is questionable in many points.

According to Musashi's own account, he was born in the province of Harima (presently the Okayama prefecture) in 1584. At the age of thirteen, he engaged in his first duel against a Shinto-ryu samurai by the name of Arima Kihei, whom he defeated. Later, at the age of sixteen, he was victorious over a competent samurai named Akiyama. This match took place in the province of Tajima (presently the Hyogo prefecture).

"PIGEON AND PLUM TREE"
Sumi-e painting by Miyamoto Musashi

"CORMORANT"
Sumi-e painting by Miyamoto Musashi

At the age of twenty-one, Musashi went to Kyoto City, which at that time was the capital of Japan. There he claims to have met several famous warriors. He was triumphant over all opponents. He then traveled to different parts of the country and engaged in over sixty combats and won them all, all before he was thirty years old. Musashi doesn't mention anything about his famous duels against the Yoshioka family or Sasaki Kojiro.

By his admission, Musashi came to reflect on his ability only after the age of thirty. He started to wonder whether or not his past victories were earned because of his skill and proper fighting strategy, or whether he won the combats one after the other simply because his opponents were weaker—vulnerable and unskillful in fighting techniques. It is clear that Musashi did not engage in combat too readily after this period. His mission was to attain knowledge and ability in fighting strategy that would eradicate the elements of chance and accident from combat victories. Lack of historical documents about Musashi's life between the ages of thirty and fifty-four make it impossible for us to know exactly what he was doing during this period. It's this element of mystery that would invite many writers to speculate and thus add to the legend of Musashi's prowess.

According to his own writing, Musashi had reached a state of true understanding of martial strategy at the age of fifty. It is much like *satori* ("enlightenment") in Zen Buddhism. Musashi was seeking the ultimate truth of martial strategy that would transcend all his other knowledge of fighting methods. He finally found it within himself. His own mind was the basis of the principle of martial strategy. When he recognized this, Musashi was able to separate himself from the world of dualism, which he talks about in his last volume, *Kū*.

After reaching enlightenment in the true meaning of the Way of martial strategy, Musashi was able to enjoy the remainder of his life devoting himself to the arts. He states that he did not need any teacher or guidance from anyone for he applied his understanding of the principle of martial strategy to whatever he attempted.

As mentioned earlier, in the biographical note about Musashi, he could have been hired by any lord, but he remained a *ronin* ("masterless samurai") for most of his life. At the age of fifty-seven, he was invited by the lord Hosokawa of Kumamoto to serve him. Musashi must have

Shigefumi Kaku

MIYAMOTO MUSASHI'S MEMORIAL
Musashi was buried here in the armor of a samurai general, as he wished.

hoped at the time that he would be able to try some of his ideas of martial strategy in the political arena as an advisor to Lord Hosokawa, who had immense respect for Musashi. His dream did not materialize.

Lord Hosokawa died one year after Musashi joined the family. As a result, Musashi lost the last and only opportunity to prove to himself and to the world that he was more than just a skillful and powerful sword fighter. It can be safely said that Musashi's greatest ambition was to become some sort of statesman or at least a samurai general who, at that rank, would have let three thousand soldiers into war. This never became a reality. However, one request was granted at the end of his life—his body was wrapped in the armored costume of a samurai general.

Earlier I mentioned that Musashi came to a realization about the truth of the principle of martial strategy and as a result, at the age of fifty, was able to unlock the secret of life. Many people, regardless of profession, come to some kind of sudden spiritual "maturity" at the age of fifty if they walk the path of life with seriousness and integrity. One comes to terms with the basic truth of the world and life itself, a kind of graduation from hard discipline and training. It goes without saying that this attainment of enlightenment does not come easily for everyone. It is reserved for those who ceaselessly strive for progress and perfection.

Musashi calls his style of martial strategy *Niten-Ichi-ryu* ("Two-Heaven-One style"), which embraces both philosophical and psychological teaching as well as actual combat techniques with swords. It was previously called *En-Mei-ryu* ("Circle-Clear style"). Subsequently, it has been called *Musashi-ryu* ("Musashi style") or *Nito-ryu* ("Two-Sword style").

The word *Niten* literally means "two heavens." In its original sense, it could have stemmed from the belief that there is always someone whom one should remember and appreciate as his or her benefactor other than heaven itself. Heaven in this case is the universe, which gives human life all its necessary ingredients. It is synonymous with nature, which provides the sources of nutrition and energy such as air, water, sunlight, and food. So it is possible to interpret *Niten* as two great elements to which one owes his or her life: great nature itself and someone to whom one owes life, and because of whose assistance one can prosper and develop.

However, it may be more appropriate to understand that Musashi's

KUMAMOTO CASTLE
Near the end of his life, Musashi lived here as a guest retainer to Lord Tadatoshi, head of the Hosokawa family.

Niten includes various juxtapositional concepts—opposites in balance—such as "life and death," "body and mind," "strength and weakness," "theory and practice," "general and soldier," "the ordinary world and the enlightened world," and "victory and defeat," as well as other similar concepts.

In an enlightened world there is no conflict between opposites. Everything is in harmony and balanced, all is one and in perfect harmony. When Musashi had finally reached self-realization he was able to transcend the dualism of ordinary life; he absorbed the Way of martial strategy.

In all so-called artistic masterpieces, there is a definite yet indescribable quality of beauty and strength. It seems that all great paintings, sculptures, and books share a certain something in common that can only be created by someone who goes through incredible training and self-discipline with full concentration and absolute belief in the self. Musashi's *Five Rings* is no exception. Here is a genius who had gone through life by the Way of the sword and, by reaching the highest stage of his art, realized that the truth of life is applicable to all facets of human life. The book is thus inspiring to all of us as we witness one who opened his own path in the wilderness of life to find an eternal resting place for the ever-striving soul.

From a practical aspect, Musashi's teaching is simple and direct: "No matter what one practices, he must always try to be superior to others." In terms of combat, of course, it means that one must always win at any cost. Indeed, Musashi insists on winning throughout his teaching. He bluntly states that defeating one's opponent is the only reason for training in the art of sword fighting. As a fighting strategist, Musashi practiced what he preached; his are not simply empty words, and as a result, his readers naturally appreciate them.

Although there are some who argue about whether Musashi was truly an exceptional fighter, the fact remains that he fought more than sixty combats and won them all. This is no mean feat, as all the opponents, regardless of their inferiority or superiority, would have been armed with deadly weapons. This is the reason why you feel a certain intensity and excitement whenever Musashi talks about the actual combats and methods of winning.

Certain Japanese historians and writers[21] have commented that

Musashi's true strength as a sword fighter should have been questioned due to the fact that Musashi seems to have avoided confrontations with the outstanding samurais of his time—Yagyu Tajima no Kami,[22] Ono Jiro-e-mon Tada-aki,[23] and others. Musashi does seem mostly to have engaged in combats with unknown warriors of his time, but one must bear in mind that part of Musashi's martial strategy is to win at all times. This means that one should never fight with someone of superior strength to oneself. According to Musashi the idea is to find an opponent whom you are sure to defeat. In spite of these criticisms of Musashi's approach, he did win more than sixty combats, so his theory is not based merely on intellectual analysis of fighting techniques.

When in high school in Japan, I had the good fortune of having a gym teacher who had been to the Olympic trials as a gymnast. Although he never made it to the Olympic Games, he was one of the best of his time. Whenever he demonstrated or spoke about gymnastic techniques, everyone was impressed. It was not so much the way he talked, but because he had gone through numerous competitions and hard training in gymnastics, his technique and style demonstrated authenticity despite the fact that he was past his prime at the time. His words were intense and meaningful. Similarly, Musashi's teaching is obviously authentic to all who strive for self-development in their chosen field, whether it be sports, art, business, industrial work, academic work, politics, or anything else. He succeeded in self-actualization through his own efforts and an unshakable belief in himself. Furthermore, he inspires others to do the same—he encourages all serious walkers of the path of life that they can be great, too.

The question which naturally follows is how can one always be a winner? Musashi answers that one must learn and master the principle of martial strategy—not just any martial strategy, but his martial strategy. He claims that if one truly understands and absorbs his martial strategy, it can be applied to any field at any time. The wisdom acquired through his martial strategy is applicable to all aspects of human life. Of course, it is no easy matter to master such a profound principle, and that is why Musashi constantly stresses the importance of practice and training in order to reach a true understanding of it. Musashi concludes every teaching with encouragement and a reminder to the reader to study hard and with serious intent.

In order to be able to apply Musashi's teaching to today's world, we must keep in mind the fundamentals of his philosophy. Today's society is particularly complicated, and at first glance it is easy to be misled into believing that there are hundreds of small independent fields of society which cannot be penetrated by outsiders because of their immense complexity and specialization. However, according to Musashi, if one truly delves into his or her work, it becomes possible to apply its principle to any other human endeavor.

There are numerous cogs—people devoting themselves to different work—which run the world. Musashi believes, and demonstrates, that one should ultimately be able to find the most basic component of the whole machine. He proves this point in a most amazing manner. There is no doubt that he was blessed with some natural ability, but he endured hard training and developed incredible self-discipline in order to transcend the fighting arts to a point where they became the tool for grasping an underlying theory that is applicable to all aspects of human society.

In his discussion of actual tools, Musashi emphasizes that quality is very important. For example, a sword is the samurai's tool and its quality might determine the owner's life or death. Musashi draws an analogy with carpentry and states that if one wants to be a good carpenter it is vital to own a good set of tools. Good tools make it possible to do a good job. In olden days in Japan, when someone was about to hire a carpenter, all he had to do was to examine the carpenter's tools to determine whether the carpenter would do a good job.

Musashi isn't saying that one must be equipped with the most expensive tools, but he stresses that one must own the tools that are best suited to oneself. One should not imitate others in selecting tools or weapons. Each person has his own strengths and weaknesses, and individual differences must be considered. This is the best way to let the person express his or her own ability and achieve full potential. As a good general knows each soldier's strengths and weaknesses and assigns position and duty accordingly, so should an employee be given an assignment according to his or her ability and aptitude.

An executive of a small company with fewer than one hundred employees once found that one of his workers was very unproductive.

The worker in question was not particularly lazy or unmotivated, but somehow he was very inefficient and unenthusiastic about his work. After having observed this individual for some time, the executive decided to move him to another position with different duties. He was pleasantly surprised by an enormous change in the employee's performance level. It was a question of the application of the right individual to the right task.

Musashi further explains the importance of "the right person in the right place." For example, a good carpenter knows how to use each material in the right place. A material that is ugly but durable should be used in places where it is not too conspicuous, such as under the floor or in the foundation, where it can function as important building material. A weak but good-looking material can be used in places where people can enjoy seeing it.

Musashi reminds us that we can look at people the same way we look at building materials. Each person's uniqueness must be respected and utilized. I once heard a professor from the University of Tokyo speak at a meeting where he emphasized that true equality and fairness means paying close attention to each person's different abilities and needs and treating him or her accordingly. A mechanical equality always creates inequity, indeed. It's difficult task, however, to ascertain each person's unique strengths and weaknesses so that each person can express his or her potential in the most effective way.

Throughout the book, and particularly in volume one, *Earth*, Musashi discusses the concept of *hyoshi*, which can be translated as "rhythm," "timing," and "tempo." None of these English words, however, conveys Musashi's meaning exactly, so I use the phrase "rhythm-timing." "Rhythm-timing" is something we all experience in life, consciously or not. It is that clear but indescribable way in which something moves, develops, or is handled. It is a force of flow that is sometimes controllable and at other times not. We often speak of "bad luck," "good luck," and "bad or good omens." A favorable rhythm-timing and an unfavorable one may become mixed at times, and sometimes the bad may overwhelm the good. There are delicate, specific rhythm-timings in life which are beyond normal understanding. We are being controlled without knowledge by such delicate rhythm-timing in daily life. There are also greater rhythm-timings that seem to control events and people in such a way that we feel helpless as finite beings.

Musashi maintains that it is not difficult to differentiate between a good rhythm-timing and a bad one. He further asserts that you can "create" a rhythm-timing that is favorable to you, depending on the situation. But it is not easy to distinguish between a rhythm-timing that can be controlled and one that is inevitable. As one continuously trains and disciplines oneself, it eventually becomes possible to realize the ultimate rhythm-timing, which Musashi calls *Kū*. It is the rhythm-timing that can be perceived by intuitive wisdom. An ordinary mind may never be able to grasp the ultimate rhythm-timing, but may feel it with a proper reflection on one's life. According to Musashi, mere technical and physical practice alone will not lead anyone to the realm of *Kū*. One must first become aware of the authentic Way, which he or she must faithfully follow.

Although Musashi himself claims that he never had a teacher of any kind, it is obvious that it is beneficial for one who strives for self-development to have a good teacher who has been enlightened as to the nature of the ultimate rhythm-timing in life. A talented student may reach a certain level eventually without guidance of any kind, but one can waste a lot of time by himself or herself. The crucial point is that one should not seek outwardly too much, as Musashi warns us, for the true source of greatness is within one's mind and spirit. Instruction and guidance from outside—whether a personal teacher, a seminar, or a book—is good to wake up the individual's potential and belief in the self, but ultimately, it is the person who brings out the greatness from within himself or herself.

Musashi is critical of those who are more interested in "having" than "being," for a life centered on "having" is a shallow existence. This does not mean, however, that Musashi denies the value of material possessions in life. On the contrary, it is said that he was always blessed with material comfort because of his outstanding skill in making various weapons and tools. This is a reflection of the pragmatism of his martial strategy. Musashi's constant awareness of the importance of rhythm timing seems to have been applied to his spiritual development, combat situations, and daily living. In a sense, he was always a winner in every facet of his life.

An ordinary rhythm-timing can be found by anyone without special training. It requires some concentration, which anyone is capable of with some effort. In the same way, many physical skills in arts and sports can be learned through constant practice. However, an ordinary rhythm-timing and the possession of many physical skills can never lead to transcendence to a higher level of existence without the ultimate wisdom based on *Kū*, according to Musashi. One must maintain self-discipline, perseverance, willpower, diligence, and a proper perspective on life in order to discover the ultimate rhythm-timing of life itself.

Now, as for Musashi's two-sword style, it is extremely well known, but its meaning is not understood by everyone. Musashi does not necessarily believe that fighting with two swords, one in each hand, is superior to the orthodox style of fighting with one sword. As a matter of fact, he himself never used the two-sword style in an ordinary combat situation of one-to-one fighting. In *Niten-ki*, it's reported that Musashi used the two-sword style against a master of the sickle-chain, Shishido Baiken.[24] Another occasion when he used the two-sword style was his combat against the Yoshioka[25] family, when he was forced to draw both swords to escape the predicament he was in. In the case of Shishido Baiken, Musashi used one of his swords to tangle up his opponent's chain and the other sword to kill him.

In explaining the reason for using the two-sword style in practice, Musashi is consistent in his pragmatism when he claims that one should not die until all weapons and means to defeat the opponent(s) have been used up. Musashi's students were encouraged to practice with a short sword in the left hand while using a regular sword in the right. Musashi theorizes that in practice it is effective for a beginner to use two swords at once, because it will strengthen the hands and arms in such a way that one can use one sword in actual combat with more power and focus. Thus, Musashi does not insist on the superiority of the two-sword style in an actual fighting situation, rather that his two-sword system makes the orthodox one-sword style more effective.

VOLUME TWO **WATER**

I call this volume *Water*, for herein I use the characteristics of water to describe the method to gain victory. It is not easy to express satisfactorily the principle of the Way in words, but I trust that it can be intuitively grasped by the reader despite the inadequacy of the words. You really must pay full attention to every word in this book, otherwise it is quite possible that you will miss the true understanding of the Way.

When you read the doctrine of martial strategy explained in terms of the one-to-one combat situation, you must extend the principles and apply them to warfare involving ten thousand against ten thousand. The uniqueness of the Way of martial strategy is that you can be misled by the slightest misunderstanding or deviation. It is not enough that you read what is written here, you must train as hard as if you were the one who developed the doctrine, instead of being the one who had it given to you. Train as constantly as if you were the source of the discovery of the Way. Avoid mere imitation or learning without sincerity. Reflect on this point and train diligently.

THE MENTAL ATTITUDE IN MARTIAL STRATEGY

In the world of martial strategy you must maintain a normal, everyday mental attitude at all times. Whether it is just an ordinary day or whether you are in a combat situation, your mental attitude should in essence be the same. One should have the feeling of being broad and straight, without being too rigid or too soft. Through total composure you must maintain mental balance at all times. You should not lose your self-control even for a moment. You must study this very hard so that you will be able to maintain a relaxed state of mind at all times.

When you are physically calm you must be mentally alert; conversely, when you are physically active, maintain a serene state of mind. In other words, your mind should not be directly affected by your body and vice versa. Be attentive at all times to all things without being overly anxious. You must maintain a gentle countenance and a sturdy state of mind. Do not let others perceive your true intentions. One who serves others should be generally aware of the overall flow of things, while one who leads should be aware of everything including seemingly insignificant matters. Regardless of the social positions people hold, everybody should sincerely respect each other as equals.[1]

Your mind should not be contaminated by any prejudice. Keep an open mind and maintain a broad perspective. It is of the utmost importance that you cultivate both wisdom and spirit. With maturity of wisdom and knowledge, you will come to know the difference between justice and injustice in the world, as well as the right and wrong of various matters in society. You should become familiar with different arts and professions, and once you become wise enough not to be easily deceived by others, you will have achieved something valuable in accordance with my martial strategy. I should emphasize that there is something unique about the concept of wisdom in my martial strategy. When you are completely occupied by the business of fighting during combat on the battlefield, it is crucial that your state of mind be immovable, and this is only possible by a thorough realization of the doctrine of martial strategy. Try to understand and appreciate this point.

POSTURES IN MARTIAL STRATEGY

In general, you should keep your head erect without leaning forward, backward, or sideways. Keep your eyes clearly focused with no wrinkles on your forehead except some furrows between your eyebrows. Without moving your eyes and without blinking, narrow your eyes slightly. Stick your chin forward a little with your nose straight and make a face that is calm and displays no disturbance.

As for your neck, keep it straight with the scruff tense. Below the shoulders, the tension should be even throughout the body, with your shoulders low, your neck straight, and without pushing your buttocks out. Tense your legs from the knees to the toes and push your stomach forward so that you do not bend at the hips. There is a method called *kusabi o shimeru* ("tighten the wedge") according to which your posture should be such that you can hold the short sword in your belt without having any slack in it.

In general, you must maintain the fighting stance in everyday life; your everyday posture must immediately become the fighting stance. You must appreciate this point and study it hard.

EYE FOCUS IN MARTIAL STRATEGY

Your eyes should be able to focus on a large and wide area. There are two kinds of seeing: *kan* and *ken*, the former being the most important and the latter less essential. In martial strategy it is crucial that you be able to keenly see objects at a great distance and that objects in close proximity be viewed with a broader perspective. In a combat situation, you must see your opponent's sword in the context of his strategy as a whole rather than observing each physical movement. You must study this point well. This method of seeing is the same for both one-to-one combat and warfare involving armies.

It is important to be able to see on either side of yourself without moving your eyes. You will not be able to do this suddenly in an emergency situation. You must try to cultivate this method of seeing in everyday life and maintain the same type of eye focus at all times. Study and train well in this matter.

HOW TO HOLD YOUR SWORD

In holding your sword it is important to place the least tension on your thumb and index finger while pressing the middle finger a little harder. The remaining two fingers should be tightly pressed on the sword. At the moment you strike your opponent with the sword your grip should not slacken at all. You must really intend to cut your opponent down when you face him with a sword in your hands. At the moment you cut down your opponent, there should not be any change in your grip on the sword. Make sure your hands do not weaken at the moment of impact. Whether you are striking, blocking, or pushing down the opponent's sword, you must maintain the same strength of grip simply by adjusting the thumb and index finger slightly. Whatever the situation, it is imperative that you always have the intention of cutting down your opponent when you hold your sword. Whether it is a practice-cutting or an actual combat situation, there should not be any change in the way you hold your sword.

In general, be careful not to become too rigid with your sword or hands. Rigidity produces a "dead hand," while flexibility is the source of a "living hand." This point must be kept in mind at all times.

FOOTWORK

As for your footwork, try to slightly raise the tips of the toes above the floor while placing your weight firmly on your heels. It is best to walk in a normal fashion, although there may be some difference in speed or size or stride depending on the circumstances during combat. I am not in favor of the three types of footwork called the "jumping footwork," the "floating footwork," and the "static foot position." It has been said, "The footwork of yin and yang is important," which means that one should not move one foot only in movements. When trying to cut down your opponent, when retreating or parrying off the opponent's attack, you must move both feet in such a way as to make the footsteps right and left, right and left. Never move just one foot all the time. This point must be understood and studied well.

THE FIVE SWORD-HOLDING POSITIONS[2]

The five sword-holding positions consist of upper, middle, lower, right side, and left side. Although we make a distinction between five different sword-holding positions, it must be kept in mind that they all have a common purpose, namely to cut down your opponent. There are no positions other than the five basic ones described here. But regardless of which position you assume, do not be caught up with the idea of the position itself; instead, you must think of cutting down your opponent.

As far as determining how big or small your sword-holding position should be, use whichever size of position is most advantageous to the situation. The fundamental sword-holding positions are upper, middle, and lower; their applications are possible on both sides. In a situation where you have an obstacle overhead or on either side, you must decide which position should be used, right or left side, depending on the predicament you are in.

It has been said that the most important of all positions is the middle one. The middle sword-holding position is the basis of all positions. Making an analogy with warfare, the middle position is similar to the general in importance. The other four positions follow the general, so to speak. One must appreciate this point well.

THE WAY[3] OF THE SWORD

Once you master the true art of the sword, you will be able to wield a sword with two fingers without difficulty. When you try to swing the sword too fast, you go astray from the authentic method and lose control. It is important that you maintain a calm state of mind when you wield your sword.

It is difficult to wield the sword if you try to treat it in the same way as you would a folding fan or short sword. A sword is different from these. When one swings a sword in a fast and small way as if it were a folding fan or a short sword, this method is called "short sword chopping." It is not effective in cutting a man down. After you have swung the sword down, bring it back in a natural and easy way to the upper position. Similarly, when you swing the sword sideways, make sure to bring it back in the opposite direction along the same sideways line. After executing a move, always bring the sword back to the original position, where you feel most comfortable. Keep your elbows straight and swing the sword vigorously. This is the Way of the sword.

By understanding the principle of the five basic sword-holding positions of my martial strategy, you will be able to wield the sword without difficulty and with precision. You must train and study this matter well.

THE FIVE SWORD-HOLDING POSITIONS— THE FIRST METHOD

The first sword-holding position is called *chu-dan* ("middle level") in which you direct the tip of your sword to your opponent's face as you confront him. As your opponent attempts to strike you, parry his sword to the right, thus controlling his movements. At his second attempt to strike you, strike down his sword. At his next attempt to strike you, attack his hand from below with your sword which you have just brought down. This is the basic technique of the first method.

In general, these five sword-holding positions are not easy to learn simply by reading what is written in this book. You must practice with a sword in your hands in order to understand the five sword-holding positions. By training in these basic positions, you will be able to develop your own particular style and, eventually, deal with any of your opponent's techniques. You will then agree that there is no other way of holding the sword than these five methods. You must practice them diligently.

THE SECOND METHOD[4]

The second method calls for you to bring your sword high above your head and as your opponent is about to strike you, execute one decisive blow at him. If you miss this first blow, leave the sword where it ends up and when your opponent tries a second attack, cut your opponent from below with a scooping motion. You can repeat this technique if your opponent persists.

There are various mental attitudes as well as rhythm-timing involved in this method of fighting. So if you concentrate on this technique as you follow the *Niten-Ichi-ryu* method and practice hard, you are bound to become invincible as a result of a true understanding of the five basic sword-holding positions and techniques. You must train diligently in this subject.

THE THIRD METHOD[5]

The third method involves striking the opponent's hand from below with your sword, which you hold as if it were hanging in your hands lightly. As you attempt to strike your opponent's hand, he may swing his sword down again, at which point you take advantage of your superior timing and cut sideways at your opponent's upper arms. By executing the technique with your sword in the lower position you stop your opponent's attack with one totally focused strike. This particular method of holding your sword is commonly practiced in both the early and later stages of one's training. It is important that one actually practice this with the sword rather than just conceptualizing it.

THE FOURTH METHOD[6]

In the fourth method of sword-holding, stand with your sword in the lower position on your left side and strike your opponent's hand from below the moment he attacks you. When you attempt to strike your opponent from below, he may try to knock down your sword. If this happens, strike your opponent in the direction of your shoulder diagonally with the feeling of striking his hands, pushing his sword in the same direction. This technique is based on the true Way of the sword. This method can also be used if your opponent tries a second consecutive strike. You must try to understand this method well and train diligently.

THE FIFTH METHOD[7]

The fifth method involves holding the sword at your right side. The moment your opponent attacks you, swing your sword diagonally upward, then bring it vertically downward. This method enables you to learn the basic sword techniques well. If you follow this method faithfully you will eventually be able to wield a heavy sword without any difficulty.

It is not actually necessary to write in detail about these basic sword-holding positions. With constant practice of these five methods you will come to understand the general fundamental techniques of my style. You will grasp the meaning of rhythm-timing as well and be able to deal with your opponent's attack effectively. During actual combat with an opponent, you can detect his movements in advance by applying this method of sword fighting and gain victory by using rhythm-timing. Try to understand this through constant practice.

THE POSITIONS WITHOUT PRESCRIBED POSITION OF THE SWORD

"The positions without prescribed position of the sword" means that there should not be any specified way of holding a sword. However, it is true that you could call the five basic sword-holding positions "specified positions." The important thing is that you must always hold the sword so as to cut the opponent in the most effective way, regardless of the situation you are in. The five basic sword-holding positions described earlier are all flexible. For example, the upper position can become the middle position with a slight change in height, depending on the situation, while the middle position can become the upper position by raising the sword slightly. Similarly, with a little alteration of height, your sword can move from a lower to a middle position. The two side positions can also change to middle or lower positions with a slight forward adjustment of the sword, depending on the situation. Thus, it can be said that there are really no "fixed" sword-holding positions. This is why we call it the "positions without prescribed position of the sword."

In facing an opponent with a sword in your hand, it is crucial that you intend to cut the enemy, no matter what. You may block your opponent's sword, you may strike it, touch it, push it, or simply parry it. But these actions are simply a setup for the main purpose of cutting your opponent down. You must remember this. When your mind is caught up with the idea of blocking your opponent's sword, striking it, touching it, pushing it, or parrying it with your sword, you may become less effective in striking down your opponent to win. You should be constantly looking for a chance to cut down your opponent and nothing else.

In the strategy of warfare involving armies, we divide the force and separate it in different groups and position them in various places, which is equivalent to the sword-holding stances in the individual combat situation. But again, the purpose of positioning the groups in different places is simply to win the battle. It is wrong to place the emphasis on forming positions. You must study and think deeply about this matter.

STRIKING THE OPPONENT IN A SPLIT SECOND

When you and your opponent are facing each other in close proximity, you must swing your sword directly at your opponent with lightning speed in order to defeat him without giving him a chance to react to your tactics. This method is called "striking the opponent in a split second." In executing this technique, you must strike your opponent while he is still undecided about whether he should pull back, parry, or strike. By faithfully training in this method you will learn how to strike your opponent in a split second without hesitation and with lightning speed.

RHYTHM-TIMING OF THE SECOND ACTION

Suppose that your opponent pulls back quickly when you try to attack him. At that moment, you should pretend to strike him at full force, making him tense up for a moment and then relax for the next. The moment he relaxes, strike him to finish. It is also an opportune moment to strike your opponent when he pulls back a little to relax momentarily.

These tactics are called "rhythm-timing of the second action."

It may be difficult to learn this technique simply by reading this book, but if you receive proper instruction and guidance from someone, you will immediately understand it.

STRIKING WITHOUT
THOUGHT AND CONSCIOUSNESS[8]

When you and your opponent are about to strike each other at the same time, maintain your physical readiness as well as mental concentration to strike the opponent. As you swing your sword down, increase the speed of the sword with a spontaneous movement of the hands without deliberate effort. This is called "striking without thought and consciousness" and it is the most important striking method; you will encounter it often. Try to learn it and train well in this method.

THE STRIKING METHOD CALLED
"FLOWING WATER"

If you face an opponent of equal ability, he may try various techniques such as a quick retreat, parrying, and dodging. In such a case, you must maintain concentration and muster all your physical and mental strength with the feeling of expanding your whole being. Swing the sword slowly and as forcefully as possible. Once you learn this technique you will have no trouble executing it. However, when using it you must be able to discern your opponent's position and ability.

STRIKING WITH PERPETUAL MOVEMENTS

As you attempt to strike your opponent, he may try to block or parry your attack. In such a case you should keep striking him continuously on his head, hands, and feet, wherever you can. In accordance with the principle of sword-fighting technique, you must strike your opponent continuously anywhere you can. This is called "striking with perpetual movements."

You must train yourself well in this method. You will encounter this technique all the time. You should learn the details of this technique by practicing with a sword in your hands.

A STRIKE CALLED "SPARKLING STONE"

When you and your opponent face each other so closely that your swords are almost touching, you should strike your opponent from where you stand without raising your sword at all. This method requires the combined strength of your legs, body, and hands as well as speed. It cannot be acquired without constant training, but it will be a powerful technique for you once you learn it.

A STRIKE CALLED "RED LEAVES"

This method involves knocking down your opponent's sword, after which you must immediately pull your sword back to its original position. As your opponent stands in front of you, indecisive about whether he should strike or simply parry your attack, you should use either the "striking without thought and consciousness" method or the "sparkling stone" and strike his sword forcefully. As you strike his sword, keep the pressure on his sword and the end of it downward. In this way, you will undoubtedly force your opponent to drop his sword.

This method can be learned well with serious training. Make sure that you will practice it well.

INDEPENDENT MOVEMENT OF YOUR BODY AND SWORD

It is not correct to move your body and sword at the same time when you execute an attacking technique on your opponent. Depending on how your opponent charges, you should assume a sword-holding stance appropriate to striking him while your sword should move independently without regard to body posture at all. It is also possible for you to strike your opponent with your sword and not move your body at all, although normally you should first assume a striking stance and then follow with your sword. Try to understand and practice this well.

THE INTENTIONAL STRIKE
AND ACCIDENTAL CONTACT

Striking with intention and focus and making a contact by accident are two different matters. When we say *utsu* ("strike"), this means that you should aim correctly and swing your sword at your opponent with the intention of striking him. This is a technique with precision and effectiveness. On the other hand, *ataru* means "accidentally striking or making a contact with your opponent" or "striking your opponent by luck." In such a case, a correct and effective technique is lacking. No matter how hard and forcefully you strike your opponent, if it was accidental and not the result of correct and well-focused technique it was merely *ataru*, even when your opponent happens to die instantly.

Utsu means striking with intent and concentration. You must understand this well. After striking your opponent's hands or legs accidentally—*ataru*—you should strike with intent and focus—*utsu*. In other words, *ataru* is in spirit merely touching and no more. Once you practice this well you will appreciate the difference between the two.

THE BODY OF AN AUTUMN MONKEY[9]

"The body of an autumn monkey" is a metaphor for not stretching your hands. In order to get close to your opponent before he attacks without extending your hands at all, you must quickly bring your whole body close to him. If you extend your hands, your body is likely to stay at a distance from your opponent, which is no good. You must drive the whole of your body close to your opponent with one quick move. Getting close to your opponent is not particularly difficult if you and your opponent are facing each other a sword's distance apart. Try to understand this well.

THE METHOD CALLED
"THE BODY OF LACQUER AND GLUE"

This is the technique of pressing your body to your opponent's so that he feels stuck to you. As you get close to your opponent in a combat situation, your whole body, including your head and legs, should move in close to his.

In many cases, people advance quickly toward an opponent with only their head and legs, leaving their body behind. You must learn how to get close to your opponent so that there is no space between you and your opponent. Try to understand this well.

MEASURING YOUR HEIGHT
AGAINST YOUR OPPONENT'S

When you get close to your opponent in a combat situation, it is important that you straighten up your hips, legs, and neck as if you were measuring your height against your opponent's. As you attack your opponent, stretch your body so that you feel taller than him. Appreciate what this teaching means and practice it well.

THE METHOD OF "BEING STICKY"

In a combat situation, when you and your opponent exchange techniques with the swords, place your sword on his as he tries to block your attack and feel as if you were sticking to it as you advance on him. The feeling of sticking to him means that your sword cannot be easily separated from his; this should be accomplished with a moderate amount of strength. As you advance on your opponent to stick your sword to his, you can do it as gently as you like.

But sticking to your opponent's sword and entanglement are two different matters. The former means you are dominating your opponent, the latter that you are weak and confused. The difference between the two must be understood well.

TACKLING YOUR OPPONENT

This means throwing your whole body against your opponent's after positioning yourself close enough to him. Turn your face slightly away and attack your opponent's chest with your left shoulder.

As you attack your opponent, maximize your total physical strength by synchronizing your breathing and timing. You should feel as if you were bouncing when you jump at your opponent. Once you master this method of tackling, you will be able to bounce your opponent back twelve to fifteen feet. It is even possible to kill your opponent with this technique. Practice this method well.

THREE TECHNIQUES OF PARRYING YOUR OPPONENT'S SWORD

The first of the three techniques is to block your opponent's sword with yours by trying to stab his eyes and thus bringing his sword toward your right shoulder. The second one is called the "stabbing block," which involves blocking your opponent's attack by thrusting your sword out and trying to stab his right eye as if scissoring his neck. The third one is used when you are holding a short sword. Do not pay much attention to the blocking aspects with this technique, just charge at your opponent thrusting your left fist at his face.

These are the three blocking techniques. It is effective to imagine that you are thrusting at your opponent's face with your left fist. Train in this method well.

STABBING AT THE FACE

As you cross swords with your opponent, it is important that you continuously move as though you are stabbing at his face, with the tip of your sword finding an opening at the moment of his attack or of yours. If you maintain your posture and your intention of stabbing your opponent's face, you can dominate your opponent. Once you are successful at controlling your opponent, there are various ways to defeat him. You must study this well.

When your opponent starts to fear that he is being controlled by you during combat, you have victory in your hands. So bear in mind that the "stabbing at the face" technique is important. You must include this as a necessary technique of your training in martial strategy.

STABBING AT THE HEART

This technique should be used when you cannot use your sword freely because of obstructions above and at both sides. In such a case, instead of cutting and striking as you would normally do, you simply stab your opponent right in the chest.

An effective method of dodging an opponent's strike is to show your opponent the vertical straight ridge of your sword, then draw your sword back without twisting it and stab at your opponent's chest. This is a useful method and should be utilized particularly when you are tired or if your sword becomes dull. Try to understand and use it appropriately.

THE KATSU-TOTSU[10] METHOD

This method is used when you are attacking an opponent and trying to subdue him while he is attempting to counterattack you. You should bring your sword up high from below, stabbing at your opponent and striking him with a reverse blow. You must execute the technique with a rhythm of high speed, shouting "Katsu!" when thrusting the sword up and "Totsu!" as you strike your opponent. This particular rhythm-timing is frequently used during combats.

An important consideration in this technique is to bring the tip of your sword upward, stabbing at your opponent, striking him with total concentration of mind and body. Try to appreciate this and train well in it.

SLAPPING-DOWN BLOCK

As you exchange blows with your opponent during combat, draw him into a particular rhythm-timing which is advantageous to you, then block his attack with a slapping gesture and immediately strike him back. The slapping motion should be executed with moderate force, it is not an actual block. Get into the rhythm-timing of your opponent's attack and just lightly slap his sword, simultaneously attacking him.

It is vital that you take as dominant a role with the slapping gesture as you do with actual striking. Once you gain control over your opponent with a rhythm-timing of slapping his sword, you can ensure with very little effort that no matter how forcefully he tries to attack you, the tip of your sword will not be pushed downward. Try to master this and examine it well.

FIGHTING MULTIPLE OPPONENTS

This method concerns a situation in which you have to deal with many opponents simultaneously on your own.[11] Drawing both your regular and short swords at the same time, stretch out your arms sideways. Try always to chase your opponents in one direction even though they may try to attack you from different angles. Try to perceive who will attack, from which direction, and in what order, and then deal with the one who comes first. After grasping the overall situation, utilize both swords at the same time in crossing motions. After cutting down one of the opponents, do not hesitate or become passive even for a moment. Instead, immediately bring the swords to your sides and as the opponents try to rush toward you, cut them down one by one and force the whole group back, thus breaking up the team. Try to be able to attack your opponents continuously as they come forward. You must try at all costs to attack them in such a way as to make your opponents form some sort of line, and as soon as they become disorderly and piled up you must attack them without hesitation. It is not very efficient to try to charge into a group of adversaries without having any specific tactics in mind. It is also not a good idea just to wait for your opponents to come forward.

You must intuitively grasp your opponent's rhythm-timing and then find a vulnerable point in the group through which you gain victory. Whenever you can, try to practice the rhythm-timing of fighting against a large group by using a large number of people available for practice. Once you get into the rhythm-timing of charging into your opponents, it will not be difficult to deal with even ten or twenty opponents at the same time. Try to understand this and train in this matter well.

THE PRINCIPLE OF COMBAT

By being aware of the principle of sword fighting you will learn how to be victorious in combat. I will not write about this in detail here. You must practice diligently in order to become familiar with the Way of victory. The principle of sword fighting is said to be the core of martial strategy. I shall instruct you directly in words on this subject.

SINGLE STRIKE

It is crucial that you should be totally determined to gain victory with a single strike. This principle is not easy to understand unless you practice my martial strategy assiduously. However, once you really master it, martial strategy will become part of you. You will be able to win any combat you choose. Practice it well.

DIRECT TRANSMISSION

The essence of direct transmission is to learn the true meaning and techniques of *Niten-Ichi-ryu* and transmit it to others. It is crucial that you should train very diligently in martial strategy. I shall instruct you personally on this matter by oral teaching.

So far I have written about the principles of sword-fighting techniques in *Niten-Ichi-ryu* in summary form. Martial strategy is the Way based on the principle of victory over others with the sword, which should be attained through practice of the five basic sword-holding positions. Your mind and body must become totally absorbed by the Way of the sword. You must learn how to cultivate wisdom, understand the rhythm-timing of the Way, become skillful in using the sword, and be able to control yourself totally at will.

According to the principle, you must be able to defeat one opponent and then two opponents, and then gradually you must learn how to differentiate between good and evil in the world of martial strategy. In order to attain the principle—and this cannot be accomplished overnight—you must learn each subject written about in this book step by step and train accordingly. From time to time, you must engage in actual combat in order to develop yourself in martial strategy as well.

You should be always mindful of the basic teaching: never be hasty; be willing to learn about the loss and gain of martial strategy through actual combats; do not be hesitant about encountering anyone; and by perceiving your opponent's mental condition you will always gain victory. It will be a long and arduous path, but you must walk it with patience and determination.

Maintain a composed attitude at all times. You must realize that it is your duty as a samurai to follow and practice the Way of martial strategy. So you must try to improve yourself every day—be better today than you were yesterday and tomorrow you will defeat someone less able than you; after that you should be able to defeat someone superior to you. Try to follow the instruction in this book faithfully and always keep your mind focused on the study of martial strategy.

Winning over many opponents may not mean anything if you betray the teaching of the true path. Once you master this principle, you will come to realize why you are capable of defeating many opponents single-handedly.

Having understood the principle of my martial strategy, both its mental discipline and physical skill, you will come to acquire the knowledge and wisdom of my martial strategy, which can be applied to warfare involving armies as well as one-to-one combat. You must train in and practice the Way of martial strategy constantly with patience, determination, and unceasing effort.

To: Terao Magonojo

May 12, 1645
Shin-men Musashi

ANALYSIS

The volume *Water* is full of concrete teachings regarding the basic techniques of *Niten-Ichi-ryu*. Musashi refers to the mental attitude of the sword fighter as he faces the opponent. He discusses the method of holding the sword, emphasizing that there should not be any specific ways that one should conform to, for the purpose is one and the same from the beginning to the end of combat—to defeat and kill the opponent(s). Musashi was surely concerned that his teachings in the book would end up as mere theory, and that is the reason he finishes each passage by saying that one should train diligently in order to digest each important principle. Musashi repeatedly writes that one must continuously train oneself and try to improve one's technique through different means and resources. Musashi warns that readers should not give up or become content with learning the techniques in a half-hearted way. He even adds that you should try to pursue the principle of martial strategy as explained in the book as if you were the one who discovered it.

When Musashi speaks of the body he refers to both mind and body, and his emphasis is placed on the concept of *heijo-shin* ("the everyday mind"). Ordinarily one imagines that one's mind-set when having a cup of tea is different from one's mind-set in combat. Not according to Musashi. He feels that when one trains and disciplines the self physically and mentally according to the Way, the mind becomes calm and stable at all times, not preoccupied with any preconception or prejudice. This state of mind, which is attained after serious and hard training, Musashi calls *heijo-shin*. It is not the mental attitude of an ordinary person but of one who has gone through extraordinary training and self-discipline. The everyday mind of an ordinary person is not called *heijo-shin*, for it is not based on the true inner strength that can be attained only through a hard and authentic training.

When one is equipped with *heijo-shin*, he can deal with both emergency and normal situations in the same manner. So Musashi is saying that one must keep *heijo-shin* whether having a cup of tea or engaging in a life-and-death battle. It is not an artificially contrived state of mind; rather, it is the natural result of true training and discipline that brings out in each person at all times the highest and most efficient mental attitude.

As for one's physical posture and stance, Musashi teaches that one should keep the spinal cord in a straight line with the neck. Lower the shoulders and push the stomach out a little. Maintain a natural facial expression with a steady eye focus. Feel steadiness from the knee to the toes and keep the hips straight and unbending.

Musashi's teaching is always concrete and goes straight to the point. Ordinarily, this type of instruction from a great master of the seventeenth century would have come to only a select few and only by a "secret method" or "special instruction."[12] But Musashi does not try to hide anything from anybody. One of the most refreshing aspects of his book is its openness, which seems to come from his absolute confidence in himself and his method. In his introductory remarks, Musashi states that he will not use any old words from Buddhist scriptures or old martial strategies. He sticks to this consistently and as a result people of entirely different ages and cultures can still enjoy and learn from him.

One of the most outstanding teachings in the volume *Water* concerns the methods of holding a sword facing an opponent. Musashi says that it should be kept in mind at all times that the correct position of holding the sword when facing an opponent is that one which will allow one to kill the opponent. The reader is reminded that it is not how to hold a sword that is crucial, but how to kill the opponent. Musashi concedes, however, that there are five basic methods of holding a sword to start with. This is purely for the sake of expediency for practice and is necessary for beginners.

As long as one has to consciously think about one's posture with a sword in one's hands while facing an opponent, one cannot win, says Musashi. An effort to maintain one particular posture with a sword in one's hands makes one's mind and body rigid and therefore unable to move freely according to the absolute need to win. In combat situations, the opponent will likely have many different techniques, both offensive and defensive, to which one must respond. In theory, and particularly during one's training, it is possible to move through a series of pre-scribed postures and stances, but in a real combat situation, this is not practical. The notion of postures and stances with a sword in one's hands must be disregarded and one must stand in front of one's opponent with only the idea of killing the opponent, or at least defeating him. In real combat, therefore, what must prevail is *heijo-shin* instead of the rigid concept of "postures and stances with a sword in hand." This is the essence of superior ability and is based on freedom of mind and body.

Let's look at an example. A karate master stood in front of an opponent whom he had never met previously. The master wanted to demonstrate correct techniques and postures becoming of a true master. The opponent moved fast and in such an irregular manner that the master was confused and unable to cope with him. Finally, the master threw away all the traditional rigid forms and let his mind flow. The result was that the master defeated the opponent without any trouble. In the beginning, the master was too conscious of his own stances and postures and his mind and body froze for a moment. When his *heijo-shin* was recovered, however, he had no problem. This is how Musashi's *heijo-shin* prevails in combat.

Another valuable teaching in *Water* is related to seeing and observing things. Musashi describes two kinds of seeing: one with the physical eye, the other with one's perception and intuition. Musashi does not underestimate the importance of the physical eye, teaching that you should train yourself to see on both sides of yourself without moving your eyeballs. This kind of seeing is called *ken*, and it makes it possible to judge the distance between the opponent and yourself. *Kan* is the mental vision that is needed to perceive things beyond their physical appearance. *Ken* is seeing things without intending to while *kan* is purposeful. Musashi advises that you should put more emphasis on *kan* than on *ken*. The essential element of things must be grasped with effort, which is the work of *kan*. The physical eyes see things without effort—this is the work of *ken*. A modern example of this point: in a business meeting it is important to understand what your opponent really thinks or anticipates from the negotiations instead of paying attention to the numbers or figures on the desk alone.

It is crucial that you should not be pushed around by your opponent; you must take the lead in any contest. In explaining the upper method of holding a sword, Musashi teaches that you should strike your opponent without hesitation while he is still attempting to attack and continuously strike at him from the lower position if you miss your first strike. Applying this point to modern-day living, Musashi's teaching suggests that you should always use your full concentration and even if your first attempt at something is not successful, you must be prepared for the next opportunity without making excuses or dwelling on the first failure. An honest criticism is important for progress, but excessive attention to one's failures makes one lose self-confidence.

In the lower method of holding a sword, the idea is to strike the opponent from the lower level with one breath, concentrating one's entire energy of mind and body. This method, metaphorically, teaches us the importance of going for what we want with all our energies, not half-heartedly. Laziness and self-pity have no place in Musashi's philosophy. Energy is always directed forward and focused on the purpose.

As for the method of holding a sword, although Musashi specifies the basic five methods, it is obvious that he does not approve of rigid "form." The five methods of holding a sword are simply basic illustrations for beginners. Musashi emphasizes that we must make the basic methods a living form that can be flexible and applicable at any time with *heijo-shin* as its basis. Just as we must learn how to draw each separate line correctly in order to draw or write, so one correct swing of the sword is enough for combat fighting if it is a "living" swing. In real life-and-death combat, he who is fixed on a certain "form" is doomed to lose, as he must always assume that the opponent will not attack with many different techniques, thus necessitating the ability to react in an infinite variety of ways. Only "living" forms that can be adapted to changing situations can save the fighter.

Musashi makes a distinction between two kinds of strikes: the chance strike and one made with intention and ability. Needless to say, striking the opponent by chance means nothing as it does not require any focus of mind and body, while striking with intention requires correct technique, focus, and power. Touching the opponent by accident or luck does not mean anything in combat situations; striking must be executed with the actual intention of killing the opponent. In modern-day kendo and karate matches, combatants just touch each other to score points. This is inevitable, of course, for Musashi speaks of the true art of fighting in life-and-death combat with deadly weapons, while modern-day kendo and karate are sports. Indeed, if Musashi were to see modern-day sporting combats, he might scoff at them.

Miyamoto Musashi is known for originating and developing
two-sword fighting system, Niten-Ichi-ryu (Nito-ryu).
Woodblock print by Utagawa Kuniyoshi

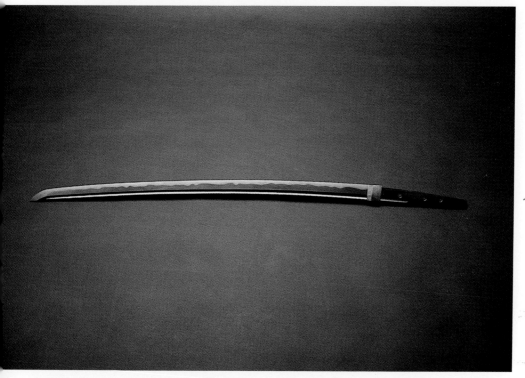

Miyamoto Musashi's *Katana* (sword). The sword represents the soul of the samurai.

Legend has it that Miyamoto Musashi fought and killed a huge lizard in the province of Echizen.

Woodblock print from the series ". . . heroes of our countries Suikoden *. . ."*
by Utagawa Kuniyoshi (c. 1834–5)

Miyamoto Musashi engaging in combat with Sasaki Kojiro on the shore of Funa Island in 1612.

Woodblock print from the series "Set of Famous Leading Heroes,"
by Utagawa Kuniyoshi (c. 1856)

"Wild Geese and Reeds"

Sumi-e painting by Miyamoto Musashi
(A pair of six-fold screens)

"Shrike on
a Twig"

*Sumi-e painting
by Miyamoto
Musashi*

The old master, Tsukahara Bokuden, parries Miyamoto Musashi's attack with a wooden pot lid. Legend has often brought together these two great masters, as portrayed in this image by Tsukioka Yoshitoshi. However, though Musashi's lifespan coincided with that of Bokuden's, it's unlikely they ever met. Bokuden died in 1572, when Musashi was 12 years old.

Woodblock print from the series "Selected Edo Color Prints,"
by Tsukioka Yoshitoshi (c. 1885)

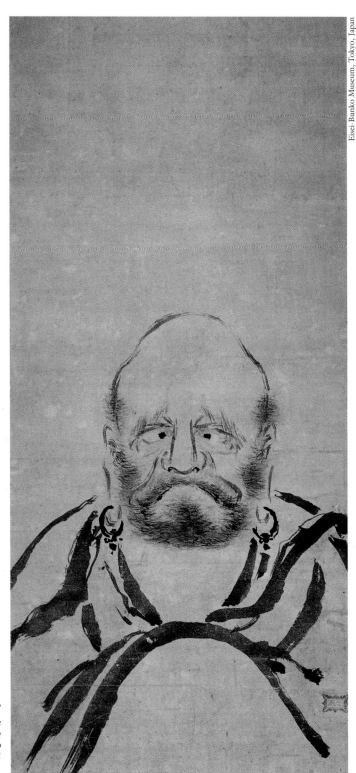

"Daruma"
*Sumi-e
painting by
Miyamoto
Musashi*

VOLUME THREE FIRE

TRANSLATION

In the *Niten-Ichi-ryu* martial strategy, the analogy of fire is used to discuss warfare involving armies. I shall, therefore, write in this volume entitled *Fire* about victory and defeat in actual battles.

First of all, in general, people demonstrate an inadequate understanding of the principle of martial strategy. For example, they exercise their fingertips or wrists in order to be able to engage in such subtle arts as the use of a folding fan. They compete to see who is fastest at moving their forearms. They also try to gain advantage by mere speed in training with a bamboo sword. They try to become skillful in hand and leg movements merely by increasing the speed of their techniques.

In my martial strategy, you must engage in actual life-threatening combats; you must become aware of the difference between life and death; you must learn the Way of the sword; you must be able to gauge the level of your opponent's ability; and you must constantly study how to defeat your opponent(s). Thus trifling matters have no place in my teaching. You will quickly find that the superficial techniques mean nothing, particularly during actual armored combat.

In my method, therefore, you must learn the fundamental Way of martial strategy through actual life-and-death battles against one, five, or even ten opponents. In principle, it follows that there should not be any difference between a victory over one opponent or over ten opponents and victory over one thousand or ten thousand. Try to understand this well.

However, from a practical viewpoint, it is not possible to bring one

"SENKI"
("WAR SPIRIT")
Calligraphy by
Miyamoto Musashi

thousand people or ten thousand people to practice together at once. So, it is important, even practicing alone, that you should try to develop your ability to perceive opponents' tactics, including strengths and weaknesses in order to overcome any opponent(s) by applying the principle of martial strategy in a correct manner. When you can do this, you will be called a true master of the Way of martial strategy. In pursuing the Way of my martial strategy you must train daily with diligence and determination. You must be so serious with intent while practicing that you make yourself believe that you are the only one in the world capable of reaching this highest level of the Way of martial strategy—and that if you do not, no one else can.

Eventually, you will attain strength and ability in the Way of martial strategy, through which you will become free from ordinary human limitations. You will come to possess even supernatural or mysterious power. This is the reason and benefit of the Way of martial strategy.

CONSIDERATION OF YOUR ENVIRONMENT

You must try to understand the environment you are in when you face an opponent in combat. For example, it is crucial that you should take a position where you can have the sun behind you. If this is not possible, then take control of the situation so that the sun is on your right-hand side.

In a combat situation inside a building, try similarly to get into a position where the light is behind you or on your right-hand side. It is important that you not have any obstruction to your rear, while also keeping your left side open for freedom of movement and the right side with limited free space. Even at night, if the circumstances allow you to see your opponent, stand with any fire behind you or place the light on your right-hand side.

Looking down on your opponent is also an important technique. Try always to occupy a position that is higher than your opponent's. In a combat situation inside a room, you should try to occupy the position usually taken by the guest of honor. Once combat starts, try to make your opponent feel as if you were chasing him to your left-hand side, placing any obstacles behind him. Above all else, try to push your opponent in the direction of any obstacles. When you succeed in chasing your opponent to an obstacle-strewn area, make sure that you do not give him a chance to look around and survey the situation. You must keep pushing him back gradually and surely without giving him a breathing space, so to speak. The same thing can be said of a combat situation inside a room, having chased your opponent back to the thresholds, lintels, doors, verandas, pillars, and so on, do not let your opponent look around and examine where he is.

In any situation, you must chase your opponent toward an area where footholds are difficult because of obstacles or to a place where there are obstacles on one or both sides. In combat, you must always try to take advantage of what your environment has to offer. Try to understand this point well and train seriously in this matter.

THREE METHODS OF DOMINATING THE OPPONENT (*SEN*)[1]

The first method of dominating the opponent is called *ken no sen* (total initiative), where you make the first move against your opponent. The second method is called *tai no sen* (waiting for initiative), which is used when your opponent makes the first move to attack you. The third one is called *tai tai no sen*, which is used when you and your opponent charge each other at the same moment. In any combat situation there are no other *sen* than these three methods. This concept of *sen* in martial strategy is a matter of primary importance as, depending on how you apply the concept of *sen*, you may win or lose the battle. There are many details which need to be taught concerning this subject, but suffice it to say that the essence of *sen* consists of beating an opponent by using the principle of martial strategy, applying it to each situation and perceiving your opponent's strategy. Therefore, I need not write about it here in detail.

Regarding the first method *ken no sen*, the following techniques are applied:

• After assuming an initially quiet posture, you suddenly execute a quick attack against your opponent.

- You show your physical strength with fast techniques while maintaining a composed frame of mind, keeping reserve power.

- Attack your opponent with one quick yet determined and forceful strike, using all your strength of mind and spirit and very fast footwork.

- Constantly dominate your opponent, with your mind free and open, until the moment of victory. These methods all belong to the first method, *ken no sen* ("total initiative").

With *tai*[2] *no sen*, try to appear weak to your opponent and wait for him to charge at you. As he comes close to you, quickly jump away and feint a lunge at him. When he displays a momentary slacking in his fighting spirit, attack him with one quick, forceful, and winning strike. Another technique of *tai no sen* occurs when you respond to your opponent's attack with even greater force. In this case, you force your opponent to lose a sense of the rhythm-timing of his mental and physical techniques for a moment, at which time you defeat him with a decisive strike. This is the principle of *tai no sen*.

In the third method, *tai tai no sen*, you respond to your opponent's quick attack with calmness. When the distance between you and your opponent becomes very close, feint a gesture of giving up. In this way, you create a lag in his fighting spirit and at that moment you attack him with a decisive winning strike. Another technique of *tai tai no sen* is to defeat your opponent with a burst of energy and spirit as your opponent tries to maintain a quiet manner of attacking you. In such a case, you should get close to your opponent and strike him with winning force by applying your mental concentration and physical strength. These are all examples of *tai tai no sen*.

It is not easy to write clearly about these matters, but you must grasp the general nature of the subject through this book and then train to acquire full understanding of the rest. These three kinds of *sen* must be employed differently depending on the circumstances. You do not always need to initiate the attack, but in a combat situation it is usually desirable to initiate the attack and put your opponent on the defensive. According to the principle of martial strategy, all tactics involving *sen* are methods of gaining victory. This must be understood and absorbed well.

THE METHOD CALLED
"PRESSING DOWN THE PILLOW"[3]

"Pressing down the pillow" refers to one's efforts not to let the head of one's opponent rise. In battles based on martial strategy, it is taboo to let your opponent take the initiative, thus putting yourself on the defensive. You must try at all costs to lead your opponent by taking complete control of him. During combat, your opponent intends to dominate you as much as you want to dominate him, so it is vital that you pick up on your opponent's intentions and tactics so as to control him. In my martial strategy, there are techniques used to stop your opponent's offensive movements just before he attempts to execute them. For example, you hold down your opponent's weapon just before he tries to thrust at you, and then you twist him away just as he is about to grapple with you. These techniques are all included in the "pressing down the pillow" method.

To further explain the "pressing down the pillow" method, it is crucial that you should perceive your opponent's intentions before they become action—you should stop your opponent just before he starts to strike. When your opponent tries to lunge toward you, stop his lunging motion just before it starts. If he intends to jump up, you stop him at his first move; if he intends to stab you with his sword, his action should not even materialize because you will stop his stabbing motion before it becomes action. When your opponent attempts techniques which are not threatening to you, let him do them. But if the techniques are dangerous to you, do not let him execute these techniques at all. The idea of stopping your opponent before his intentions become action is very crucial in my martial strategy.

However, it is not correct to be so occupied with reading your opponent's movements that you become too passive in the fighting itself. You can only become a true master of martial strategy through hard and arduous training, but once you become one you can conduct yourself freely according to the principle of martial strategy. Without conscious effort, you will be able to control your opponent so that you let him execute useless techniques whenever he wants while at the same time controlling him by using the "pressing down the pillow" method whenever you need. This subject should be studied well.

OVERCOMING ADVERSE SITUATIONS

In an effort to cross the ocean, there may be a time when one has to go over a swift current, or a long distance, crossing hundreds of miles. Both are considered quite difficult and challenging, and they require extra effort and strength. During the course of one's life many challenging situations are likely to occur, similar to crossing the ocean. In the case of crossing the ocean, the boatman must know the sailing route well. Furthermore, he must know how to judge weather conditions, as he may decide to sail alone with the help of a tailwind on the basis of his judgment. If the weather were to change suddenly and the wind take an unfavorable direction, the boatman must be prepared to finish his journey by rowing several miles with extra determination and effort.

With the same resolved attitude, you must try to overcome life's difficulties and challenges. There is also such a thing as overcoming adverse situations in martial strategy battles. In combat, you must be able to deal with difficult and challenging situations by using the principle of martial strategy, just as a skillful boatman will successfully cross the ocean by overcoming adverse conditions. You must be able to judge your opponent's ability and resources as well as your own strengths and weaknesses in the same manner as a boatman must be familiar with all conditions pertaining to sailing.

Once you overcome an adverse situation, you can relax a little. Your opponent may feel weaker or inferior by your overcoming a difficult situation, while you will feel superior. In such a case, victory is certainly yours. In both one-to-one combat situations and warfare involving armies, the concept of overcoming adverse conditions is valuable. You must study it well.

ASCERTAINING YOUR OPPONENT'S CONDITION

In the case of battles between armies, it is vital that you ascertain whether the enemy's spirit is full of, or lacking in, energy and enthusiasm. You must be able to ascertain the size of your enemy as well as their tactics.

You should also closely follow your enemy's movements. According to the principle of martial strategy, you should be able to deal with any attack that your enemy may try. You must be able to deal with the enemy by foreseeing their tactics and by dealing with their maneuvers effectively.

In one-to-one combat, it is also crucial to observe closely your opponent's movements and techniques in order to be able to judge his general ability. It is important to ascertain your opponent's strengths and weaknesses by executing techniques which he does not expect. You must perceive the highs and lows in your opponent's fighting spirit as well as the rhythm-timing of the combat situation itself so that you can execute effective techniques and apply *sen*. If you develop your ability to judge well,[4] ascertaining both your opponent's state of mind and how the combat is progressing will not be difficult. Once you achieve a state of proficiency in martial strategy, you will be able to see into your opponent's mind and come up with tactics to defeat him. Study this matter well.

THE METHOD OF "TREADING ON THE SWORD"

"Treading on the sword" is a common occurrence in martial strategy. In warfare involving armies, normally the enemy first shoots guns and arrows and then tries to execute other tactics. If you are simply reacting to your enemy's arrows and guns, spending time preparing to shoot after your enemy attacks, it may be too late to actually attack them. You must be prepared to attack your enemy as they shoot their arrows and guns so as to render the enemy incapable of using them anymore. In other words, you must tread on your enemy's action, so to speak, in order to dominate your enemy and win the battle.

In one-to-one combat, you can also render your opponent's action ineffectual by treading on his attack. You must attack your opponent immediately after his attack so as to make his follow-up attack impossible. You can accomplish this by treading on his action. Try to study and practice this well.

By "treading," I mean that you should try to suppress your opponent's follow-up techniques with your mind and body as well as your sword. The main point in "treading" is to make sure that your opponent cannot have a chance for a second technique.

The notion of *sen* is included in the treading method. You should not confuse "treading" with the idea of "exchanging blows" with your opponent at the same time. Instead, you must follow each action of your opponent as if you were sticking to your opponent. Try to understand this point and study it well.

RECOGNIZING COLLAPSE

Collapse occurs everywhere and in everything. Whether it be a house or an enemy, collapse can occur because of a lack of harmony in rhythm-timing. In warfare involving armies, it is crucial that you charge into the enemy before you lose the opportunity provided by the enemy's loss of balance and stability due to their breakdown in rhythm-timing. This is a chance to cause your enemy's collapse. If you do not take full advantage of the opportunity to defeat your enemy when they are off balance, they may regain strength and fighting spirit.

In one-to-one combat situations, too, your opponent can lose his rhythm-timing and show signs of collapse. If you miss that moment's opportunity of defeating him, he may regain his balance and renewed strength, which will make it harder to defeat him. Therefore, it is very important that you take advantage of the first signs of your opponent's collapse and not let him renew his strength. When chasing an opponent who is off balance, a straight attack with a powerful strike is effective. You must finish your opponent completely[5] so that he does not regain energy or strength and get back on his feet again. This tactic of striking your opponent to finish him is important and you should study it well. If you do not incapacitate your opponent, your final blow was not good enough. Study this well.

PUTTING YOURSELF IN THE ENEMY'S PLACE

This means that you must think of your opponent's situation. People are likely to think of a burglar as a formidable enemy when the burglar is trapped in the house during the act of burglary. But just think about it, if you put yourself in the burglar's position, how would you feel, knowing the whole world is after you? His mind is full of uncertainty and fear about being caught. In a way, he is forced to become the pheasant while others assume the role of the hawk, surrounding the house and waiting for an opportune moment to catch the pheasant—the burglar. Study this well.

In warfare involving armies, one also tends to think of the opposition as being greater than it actually is. Consequently, one becomes hesitant and executes tactics out of fear and apprehension. One should not be worried about the enemy as long as one is equipped with a well-trained army and sufficient knowledge of military instruments, as well as a method of gaining victory over the enemy.

Consider a similar situation in one-to-one combat. If you have to face a master of martial strategy who has true understanding and skill in fighting, you are likely to become afraid of your opponent and will lose confidence in your ability to win even before combat starts. Study this matter carefully.

LETTING GO OF THE GRAPPLING POSTURE (MAKING A FRESH START)

When you and your opponent are dragging on the fight in a particular posture, each knowing the other's intentions, combat is not likely to end for a long time. In such a case, it is important that you completely change tactics in order to open the door to victory.

The same can also be said of a warfare involving armies. When the battle drags on, it may produce many unnecessary casualties. In such a situation, it is vital that you abandon your old tactics and come up with a completely new method of dealing with the enemy. The same thing applies to one-to-one combat. When there is no clear sign of an end to the combat between you and your opponent, you should immediately change your tactics by adopting a new and unexpected technique in order to overwhelm him. As you deal with your opponent, you should constantly pay attention to his state of mind as well as his physical condition so that you can defeat your opponent by a technique that he would never expect. Try to understand this matter well.

THE METHOD CALLED "MOVING THE SHADOW"

When it is difficult to perceive your opponent's fighting plan, the method called "moving the shadow" can be used. In warfare involving armies, when you are unable to detect the enemy's tactics, it is effective to feint an aggressive move on the enemy in order to make them reveal their plans. Once you find out what the enemy is planning, you can then use an appropriate tactic to win, implementing the *sen* method.

In the case of one-to-one combat, when your opponent does not show his intentions by holding his sword beside or behind him, you can always make him reveal his true intentions by suddenly faking a movement. Once you realize what his combat plan is, you can effectively deal with it to defeat him. However, if you are careless in observing his movements, you may miss the opportunity of winning. Study this point well.

THE METHOD CALLED "PRESSING DOWN THE SHADOW"

When you clearly grasp your opponent's plan of attack you can use the method called "pressing down the shadow." In warfare involving armies, as the enemy attempts to attack you, respond with an aggressive maneuver. The enemy will be forced to change their tactics because of your strong response. At this point, you too should calmly change your tactics and win by using the *sen* technique.

In one-to-one combat, when your opponent makes an aggressive move, you should respond with an even stronger movement and suppress his fighting spirit. Once your opponent ceases his aggressive move as a result of your strong and effective technique, find your own good rhythm-timing and defeat him with the *sen* concept. Train well in this matter.

THE CONCEPT OF "CATCHING"[6]

The notion of "catching" (*utsuraseru*) applies to many things: yawning and sleepiness, for example. Time can also be "catching." In a large-scale battle, when the enemy is restless and trying to bring a quick conclusion to the battle, pay no attention. Instead, try to pretend that you are calm and quiet with no urgent need to end the battle. The enemy will then be affected by your calm and easy attitude and become less alert. When this "catching" occurs, quickly execute a strong attack to defeat the enemy.

You can also make yourself appear relaxed and nonchalant in one-to-one combat so that your opponent will be "caught" by the same mood. As soon as you see that your opponent has "caught" your mood, execute a decisive attack and win the battle. There is also a concept called "making one drunk," which is similar to the notion of "catching." You can make your opponent feel bored, carefree, or feeble spirited. You should study these matters well.

MAKING THE ENEMY NERVOUS AND UPSET

It is possible to make others feel upset and uneasy over a variety of things. Firstly, danger makes one nervous and upset. Secondly, feeling that a situation is hopeless or too difficult makes one nervous and upset. Unexpectedness is the third situation. You must study these things well.

In warfare involving armies, it is important that you make the enemy feel unsettled and unsafe. It is crucial that you execute an exceptionally aggressive and strong attack where the enemy least expects it. Before they make up their mind what to do and how to react to the attack, you must apply the concept of *sen* and defeat the enemy.

In one-to-one combat, you should deliberately appear slow and carefree in the beginning, and then upset your opponent with a sudden powerful attack, thus taking control of the situation and winning the battle. Try to understand and study this well.

THE FRIGHTENING METHOD

It is not unusual for people to be frightened by different things. For example, an unexpected happening is frightening. In large-scale army warfare, it is possible to alarm and frighten the enemy by different means, not merely limited to the visible. For example, it is effective to scare the enemy with noise or by creating an illusion of something large with a smaller object, and threatening them from unexpected directions.

By taking advantage of the enemy's fright and alarm, you can win through the principle of martial strategy. Also, in one-to-one combat, you can induce fear or cause alarm in your opponent by using different body postures and movements, utilizing your sword, voice, or other things which your opponent may not expect from you. At the moment of your opponent's alarm and fear, you execute a sudden attack and defeat him decisively. Try to understand and study this well.

COVERING AND SMEARING
YOUR OPPONENT

When you and your opponent engage in close-range combat and there is no sign of a decisive end, you must bring yourself in close to him as if you were smearing him with your own body. You must then find an effective way of defeating him while you cover him with your body.

In both army warfare and one-to-one combat, it is not easy to bring the conflict to an end by facing each other from a distance, constantly checking each other's movements. In such cases, it is effective to get close to your opponent as if you were smearing him with your whole body. While you and your opponents are stuck together, struggling, you must find a solution for victory. Study and train hard in this matter.

ATTACKING PARTICULAR PARTS

It is not easy to deal with a strong enemy directly from the front. In army warfare it is vital that you should attack the most noticeable or outstanding parts of an army to make the whole crumble. When this particular part of the army becomes weak, it is just a matter of time before the whole unit disintegrates. As you notice the whole army becoming weak, concentrate on attacking the most obvious and visibly apparent parts ceaselessly.

Also, in one-to-one combat, it is important to remember that you can defeat your opponent by attacking one particular part. By weakening him at one vital spot, the whole body will become weak. It will be easy to win if you take advantage of the gradual collapse resulting from damage done to one part of his body. Make sure that you study this well and find a means to win at any cost.

CONFUSING THE OPPONENT

It is crucial that you not let your opponent feel secure and confident. In army warfare, you must first perceive your enemy's plan, then by applying the method of martial strategy, you must confuse the enemy about where you will attack from, what tactics you are going to use, and even whether you are going to attack quickly or slowly. Once the enemy becomes confused, do not miss this opportunity to defeat him. This tactic must be well understood.

In one-to-one combat, it is also important that you confuse your opponent by pretending to execute various techniques, such as thrusting one moment and then lunging the next. By creating a state of confusion in your opponent, you will easily win. This is of the utmost importance to my martial strategy.

THREE COMBAT SHOUTS

The three combat shouts consist of the beginning shout, the middle shout, and the post-combat shout. It is important to use the appropriate shout for each different situation. The combat shout generates a feeling of energy and enthusiasm within the person who shouts. These are the shouting sounds used against fire, wind, and waves. The combat shouts demonstrate one's fighting spirit. In large-scale combat involving armies, it is effective to use loud sounds at the beginning of a battle, while lower and more forceful sounds should be used during the battle. The final shout is made when victory is achieved and should be loud and forceful. These are the three combat shouts.

In one-to-one combat, shout *"E-i"* (pronounced like the *"ei"* in *"eight"*) just before executing an attack on your opponent so as to jolt him, then wield your sword. In order to let others know of your victory, you should shout when the battle is over. This is called *sengo no koe* ("the post-battle shout"). It is not necessary to use any loud shout when executing a sword technique. If you shout during combat it should be low and used to harmonize your fighting rhythm with your opponent's movements. You must study this well.

BLENDING INTO THE ENEMY

In army warfare, as your army faces the enemy and the enemy appears powerful, try to attack the enemy in one particular spot. If you are successful in crumbling that particular spot, leave that spot and attack the next, and so on and so forth, as if you were going down a winding road.

This idea of "blending into the enemy" is also useful when you have to fight many opponents on your own. Try to attack one particular opponent, then choose another opponent worthy of your attention. Attack one opponent after another, feeling as if you were going down a winding road. Constantly observe all of your opponents; be aggressive at all times and do not falter during combat until you have achieved victory.

Also, when you have to deal with a strong opponent in one-to-one combat, you should basically use the same idea and constantly attack him from different directions until he crumbles. In short, the concept of "blending" represents a constant, aggressive, and determined attack to defeat your opponent by staying close to him. Try to understand this well.

CRUSHING YOUR OPPONENT

This means that you overwhelm your opponent with the intention of completely destroying him.

As you face the enemy in a large-scale battle involving armies (whether they be large or small), if you find a weak point or any disorderliness in the enemy, you must attack aggressively and crush them. If you do not totally destroy the enemy they may regain strength and come back. Just think of crushing something in your hand; the same idea can be applied to completely defeating your opponent.

In one-to-one combat, when you confront an inferior opponent or when the opponent is off-balance in his fighting rhythm-timing or is passive, you must attack him vigorously, without hesitation and without looking into his eyes, and completely defeat him. It is important that your opponent should not be able to regain strength at all to fight back. Appreciate this teaching and study it well.

CHANGING TACTICS COMPLETELY[7]

This means that you should not repeat the same techniques many times during combat. The same technique can be executed twice at most, but never more than that. Having failed in your first attempt, you may try the same technique once more. But after the second attempt, you should try a completely unexpected technique against your opponent. If this fails, you should follow it with another different technique. (Your techniques should have as much variety as the mountains and the oceans.)

It is important to maintain an element of surprise by changing your techniques from time to time. Give your opponent the sea when he expects the mountains, and vice versa. This is the Way of martial strategy. Study and practice it well.

BREAKING THROUGH THE BOTTOM

A situation could arise wherein you believe you have completely defeated your opponent physically but you have not defeated his fighting spirit. In other words, your opponent's mental self has not been defeated yet, which means he could regain his physical strength and fight back. In such a case, you must renew your spirit and attack your opponent again to ensure that he is completely defeated, with no fighting spirit or ability left. "Breaking through the bottom" must be accomplished with the sword as well as the whole body and spirit. This is not easy to master.

Once your opponent has completely crumbled, physically and mentally, you won't have to worry about him any longer. But, if this is not the case, you must be careful. If your attack is not completely thorough, it is difficult to finish off your opponent. It is important to train in this "breaking through the bottom" technique in both army warfare and one-to-one combat.

REFRESHING THE MIND

When you and your opponent are engaged in combat which is dragging on with no end in sight, it is crucial that you should come up with a completely different technique. By refreshing your mind and techniques as you continue to fight your opponent, you will find an appropriate rhythm-timing with which to defeat him.

Whenever you and your opponent become stagnant, you must immediately employ a different method of dealing with him in order to overcome him. The same thing can be said about army warfare. It is not difficult to understand this point through the principle of martial strategy. Study it and practice hard.

THE METHOD CALLED
THE "RAT'S HEAD AND HORSE'S NECK"

When you and your opponent are fighting indecisively and face a deadlock, it is crucial that you should alter the focus of your attention from the small technical details to a larger perspective. (The difference is like that between the head of a rat and the neck of a horse.) This is one of the important Ways in martial strategy.

A samurai should apply this principle to everyday living. The same technique can be used in both army warfare and one-to-one combat. This subject should be studied well.

A COMMANDER CONTROLLING A SOLDIER

You must be able to manipulate the enemy's movements as if they were your own soldiers. By applying the principle of martial strategy and executing the appropriate techniques, it is possible to control the enemy soldiers as if they were your own who fully obey your command. Study this matter well and practice it.

RELEASING THE HILT OF YOUR SWORD

There are various meanings in releasing your hand from the hilt of your sword. For example, you could mean to win without resorting to your sword. It could also mean that you would prefer to resolve the conflict without sword fighting. It is not easy to write about various things pertaining to this subject so that you understand them. Train well in this matter and you will come to understand it.

TO BE AS IMMOVABLE AS A HUGE ROCK

By studying and training in the Way of martial strategy, you will eventually become invincible, not intimidated by anything or anyone. You will become as immovable as a huge rock in your mental attitude (because of the absolute confidence that you come to possess). I will explain it to you in words directly in person.

Thus far, I have written about *Niten-Ichi-ryu*, about matters which have concerned me daily. As this is the first time I have written about them, naturally, some have not been very systematically presented. Nonetheless, what I have written about here should certainly be helpful to those who wish to follow the Way of martial strategy.

I have dedicated myself to the study of martial strategy from the time of my youth. I have trained in everything pertaining to sword-fighting techniques and have become familiar with different disciplines. As I observed teachers of other styles, it became obvious to me that they have rationalized things so that people will enjoy listening to them. Or else they practice fancy and superficial techniques for the sake of impressing others. They do not seem to abide by the truth of martial strategy.

Of course, if you were only interested in training your body and mind to a certain degree, these "untrue" methods could work up to a point. But eventually you will suffer from the ill effects of "untrue" training because it lacks substance. The true Way of martial strategy will not survive if people continue to adhere to "untrue" ways.

According to the principle of my martial strategy, you must learn the true method of sword fighting with which you will be able to win your combats. Your victory is assured with constant training and discipline in the doctrine and method of my martial strategy.

To: Terao Magonojo   May 12, 1645
                                       Shin-men Musashi

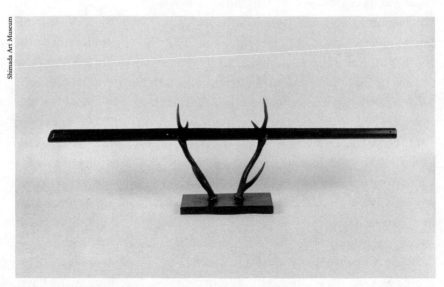

Shimada Art Museum

Miyamoto Musashi's Bokuto (wooden sword)

ANALYSIS

This volume reflects the idea of "fire" in battles. It is the application stage of the theories and techniques that Musashi speaks of in the previous volumes. He describes various combat situations and warfare in which one can find opportunities to apply what was said in the volume *Water*. One of the most important aspects of this volume is that Musashi attempts to expand the techniques and theories of one-to-one combat to include warfare involving armies. Musashi claims that if one can defeat ten opponents on one's own, the same strategy can be applied to one thousand men against ten thousand opponents.

Before we discard Musashi's theory as too simplistic, let's examine it for a minute. If you increase ten opponents by one thousand times you will have ten thousand opponents. But what about the individual? Is it possible to have one thousand warriors who can perform like Musashi? Of course not. So where would you find Musashi in the case of one thousand warriors defeating ten thousand opponents? The answer is clear, he would change his position from that of a soldier to that of a leader who commands one thousand in the defeat of ten thousand opponents. This explanation is consistent with Musashi's never-ending dream of becoming a samurai general who would lead a large group of soldiers in the event of war.

It has already been established that Musashi's martial strategy is based on his own experience and not merely theory. He teaches that one should be ready to go through actual life-and-death combat at any time.

One can only learn the true method of sword usage in serious battle where there is an imminent risk of death. One must constantly keep in mind that the only purpose of training in martial strategy is to defeat the opponent(s). Musashi also warns that one should not show off meaningless and fancy tricks or techniques to others.

It is significant that Musashi's concept of the enemy includes the places and conditions that one must deal with when facing an opponent. How to take advantage of different things around you and the vulnerability of the opponent is very important to Musashi's strategy. It is based on the idea that basically you and your opponent are equal in fighting ability per se and that what makes you superior to your opponent is your ability to manipulate the conditions presented to you, which are infinitely changeable. Of all conditions, the place where you stand to face your opponent is the most important. You must chase your opponent toward an area where there are some obstacles and make him feel unsafe standing close to them.

Musashi's teaching of *sen* is also important, although it does not originate with him. He talks about three kinds of *sen*: *ken no sen*, *tai no sen*, and *tai tai no sen*. *Ken no sen* refers to moving suddenly on the offensive after initially facing your opponent in a calm and quiet manner. When you want the opponent to act first and then react to his action, this is *tai no sen*. The third kind of *sen*, *tai tai no sen*, involves both parties attacking each other at the same time, while you take control of your opponent by finding an opening to overcome him. No matter how you happen to fight your opponent, you must control the situation and opponent in order to win the battle.

It is clear that much of Musashi's martial strategy is based on psychological and mental strategy. If you and your opponent are similarly skilled in swordsmanship, the crucial difference is the psychological makeups of both fighters. For example, Musashi writes about the principle called *makura o osaeru* ("pressing down the pillow"), which means that you should not let your opponent bring up his head. In other words, you should make sure that you have absolute control over him from the beginning to the end of the combat. In a concrete sense, this means that you must suppress the opponent's techniques before he has a chance to put them into action: if your opponent is about to jump, make sure that he can't; if your opponent shows the intention of making an aggressive attack, make sure that you stop his action before it begins.

Throughout *The Book of Five Rings*, the importance of one's mental strength is repeatedly emphasized in different forms. Physically speaking, all human beings are more or less the same, with two arms and two legs. The mind, however, is another matter: it can expand in an infinite number of ways, and it is this capacity which enables one to find a way of overcoming an adversary. Needless to say, Musashi constantly stresses the importance of physical training as well. His ideal objective is to harmonize superior physical skill with an enlightened mind, which would make one truly invincible.

Another interesting psychological strategy that Musashi writes about is *utsuraseru* ("let the opponent catch a certain feeling or mood"). If you pretend that you are tired or lazy by moving slowly, your opponent somehow will also become like that. As soon as you perceive that the opponent has become slow and weak in movement, you must attack him suddenly and forcefully to gain a victory. It is easy to relate to this principle by thinking how sleepy we become, without being conscious of it, just by looking at someone who appears sleepy. An atmosphere, feeling, or mood can indeed often be contagious.

This principle, which is part of Musashi's martial strategy, is again applicable to modern-day situations. For example, during a meeting, it is not difficult to deliberately make someone angry and lose their faculty of reasoning. You can then quickly take over the meeting by a coherent, calm, well-planned approach.

The principle of *sen* can be applied in many different ways in our lives as well. Going back to the example of the meeting, if there are no opinions being presented, go ahead and speak presenting conclusions to your advantage. If a variety of opinions are being presented, let others speak first and then at an opportune moment assert yourself with a strong opinion and bring the meeting to a conclusion with the advantage on your side. If your negotiating opponent is an assertive type of person, let him speak, pretending that you are a passive type, and then suddenly express your views with force to capture the lead in the negotiations.

Musashi speaks of the importance of crushing the opponent's fighting spirit at the very first move. One should not let the opponent feel even for a moment that he has a chance to win over you. Furthermore, Musashi's pragmatism does not lose sight of concrete advice such as placing yourself in the position where the sun shines behind you and not letting yourself be pushed into a crowded place. Musashi also writes that it is advantageous to stay in a higher place than in a lower place in combat. In his famous duel against Sasaki Kojiro, Musashi is said to have positioned himself in such a way that the sun shone behind him, thus putting Kojiro at a disadvantage.

According to Musashi's martial strategy, for the sake of winning, the end will justify the means. This amoral attitude may not be accepted in the modern world without qualification. One must understand the social background from which Musashi came. It was an age when survival was an individual's basic goal. Also, the meaning of winning and losing was somewhat different. Winning meant to live and losing meant to die. Musashi, therefore, teaches his readers to do everything possible to win. One may try to anger, scare, or confuse the opponent. A psychological tactic is just as useful and crucial as a physical one.

Musashi's *utsuraseru* refers to a method in which you entice your opponent into following your own pace and then suddenly you make a winning attack. Another tactic, *yowaseru* ("make one drunk"), suggests that you create the illusion of being easy, gentle, and relaxed. When your opponent gets lulled by the atmosphere, then you can suddenly attack and defeat him.

Musashi's teaching shows us how important it is to be able to adjust ourselves to changing circumstances. One must be flexible enough to be able to flow with the changing tide. This does not mean that one should sacrifice or relinquish one's moral principles. One's spiritual center must remain the same and one may only vary its application according to the timing and the tide of the situation. Musashi teaches that one of the most effective techniques in martial strategy is a sudden attack after luring away your opponent's attention. He gives a very concrete example: let the opponent think of a mountain while you act like the ocean, and vice versa. Musashi's metaphor is direct, simple, and effective.

According to *Niten-ki* and other stories about Musashi, he often appeared late at the site of a duel, thus trying to confuse and irritate his opponent. However, when he met the Yoshioka family he employed an entirely different tactic by showing up early and waiting for the enemy at the site. It is good to change tactics in any game or competitive sport so that the opponent becomes confused. Especially against an opponent of equal skill and strength, changing tactics is very effective.

The word *Soto-Goshu*,[8] means that one must be able to change one's thinking pattern 100 percent without any hesitation or imbalance. Similar to the previous tactics of changing thinking patterns, in *Soto-Goshu* ("a rat's head, a horse's neck") one changes one's approach radically, as if from a rat's head to a horse's neck. The implication of this thinking in the modern-day world is important as well. We live in a world of specialization, and it is easy for us to lose our sense of perspective about the true meaning of jobs and daily living in terms of the whole society. By using the *Soto-Goshu* concept, we can look at something from an entirely different viewpoint and then things become clearer and we can gain a better perspective on our lives.

Regarding *ki-ai* (shouting), Musashi says that it should initially be as loud and strong as one can make it, but that during the battle it should be lower. At the end of the battle it is used to announce the victory to others. In traditional form of karate practice, we also use different sounds for *ki-ai* according to which techniques are used and for what purpose: at the moment of the thrust one should shout *"E-i!"*; as one blocks it should be *"Ya!"*; a counterattack should be accompanied by the sound *"Toh!"* and the final attack by *"Kah!"* The combat itself changes constantly, according to which one must adjust oneself in order to execute different techniques with appropriate mental strength and *ki-ai*. In other words, your total awareness is present at all times, but you change constantly in order to accomplish the goal—to defeat the opponent. Understanding this concept in a modern-day perspective, let's take the example of making a plan for a trip. There is nothing wrong in making a well-planned schedule for a trip, and in many cases it is a must. But a meticulously planned trip can also be uninteresting. The basic principle of constant change in all things, including ourselves, cannot be ignored.

Musashi's explanation of "occupying the enemy's position"[9] is also interesting and instructional. It means that you should mentally put yourself in the position of others as a means of better understanding them. In the principle of martial strategy there is a saying that one cannot lose a battle if one knows both oneself and the enemy. Knowing oneself is a different matter entirely from knowing others, and "occupying the enemy's position" is an effective way of getting into one's opponent's head. One can perceive the opponent's intention by leading him into a certain move or position. It is also possible to know the opponent's thinking pattern by observing his reaction when attacked at vital spots. In short, it is important that one should try to think of the situation from the opponent's standpoint.

Applying the concept of "occupying the enemy's position" to modern living provides an important lesson for us all. For example, the word "kindness" is often misused in modern society. True kindness is not charity or mere sympathy for others. Kindness can be better understood as empathizing with the predicaments and emotions of others. In this sense, we do not see real kindness in our society. If we all tried to understand each other's predicaments and feel each other's emotions, there would be a lot less conflict and strife among us. Musashi also stresses that one should try to know people well in order to be able to lead them.

One of Musashi's favorite expressions is *iwao-no-mi*, which is an unshakable attitude of calmness and confidence which one has cultivated through hard and constant training in martial strategy. One can only attain *iwao-no-mi* as the result of the highest level of discipline of mind and body. There is an interesting anecdote concerning this. When asked by Lord Hosokawa to explain its meaning, Musashi simply told one of his disciples, Terao Kumanosuke, to commit hara-kiri right in front of the lord and Musashi, without any reason or explanation. Upon receiving the order, Kumanosuke prepared at once to kill himself, without hesitating or flinching for even a moment. Of course, he was interrupted before he actually killed himself. Then Musashi pointed to Kumanosuke's calm, quiet manner, a man who had just been told to kill himself for no apparent reason, and said that this was the true expression of *iwao-no-mi*.

Another anecdote explaining *iwao-no-mi* concerns an accomplished warrior who had reached the highest stage of the art of sword fighting. Having been enlightened as to the true meaning of the art of sword fighting, which should be based on the promotion of well-being of people rather than the destruction or killing of others, this great master was not interested in fighting any longer. His ability in the art of sword fighting was absolutely unquestionable; he was respected and feared by everyone. He walked the streets with a cane like a bored old man and yet wherever he went people looked at him with intense fear and respect. People were careful not to anger him and the old man was nonchalant. This is akin to having a huge rock hanging above a mountain path. People are afraid of the rock, which they believe may come down at any moment, and so they walk quietly and carefully under the rock. But the rock is actually very stable, being planted in the ground so deeply that it will never fall down. But people do not know it, and they continue to fear that it will fall down if they make any kind of loud noise as they walk under it. The rock just sits there completely indifferent to its surroundings and to people's fear and awe.

The person who possesses *iwao-no-mi* does not always just sit and watch others. If compelled, he will demonstrate his incredible strength in combat situations. His peaceful attitude is based on absolute confidence in himself. He may detest violent confrontation, but he does not fear it. In modern times, this attitude of immovable strength can be attained through serious meditation and constant self-reflection. It can be applied to sports, art, and business in different forms than those that were seen in olden times. No matter what field of human endeavor one deals with, a person with *iwao-no-mi* can demonstrate his or her potential in the most effective way.

Musashi also writes in the volume *Fire* about *soko o nuku* ("breaking through the bottom"). It is the concept of beating the opponent so completely that the opponent becomes helpless and there is no longer any danger of any counterattack. In sword fighting this often meant death for the opponent. When applied to modern situations this concept can be helpful for those in politics or business. A leader of one country that experienced an attempted coup d'etat decided to put to death all those who were associated with the attempt. This sounds unnecessarily brutal, but the leader of that country believed he was just performing his duty as head of state. He had to make sure that there would be no further attempts by anyone to overthrow his government. Musashi would have approved his action, as it was in accordance with his philosophy of *soko o nuku*. Needless to say, this analysis concerns only Musashi's martial strategy, and I am not commenting on any form of government or people's right to protest it. Musashi's society did not enjoy a democratic form of government, and his view is entirely based on his observation of his feudalistic era.

Musashi concludes the volume *Fire* by emphasizing that there is no other purpose in *kenjitsu* ("the method of sword fighting") than winning over the opponent. By following his teaching faithfully, he claims, and by practicing what is taught in this book, one can become invincible in combat. The great warrior also stresses the importance of maintaining an attitude of honesty and sincerity at all times when practicing and training in martial strategy. If your intentions are pure and honorable, your inner energy will automatically spring up and propel you in the direction of greatness. But when your thoughts are clouded with evil ideas or viciousness toward others and society in general, you will become ineffective whatever the field of pursuit.

VOLUME FOUR **WIND**

TRANSLATION

I t is important to get acquainted with other styles. Therefore, I will write about matters pertaining to other schools and styles here and will call it *Wind*.

Without some knowledge of other schools and styles, you cannot truly comprehend the Way of *Niten-Ichi-ryu*. There are those styles which emphasize strength and insist on a large sword and only practice techniques relating to the large sword. On the other hand, there are those who stress the superiority of a short sword and so concentrate on those techniques in their teaching. Yet other styles take pride in teaching as many different techniques as possible, calling various basic sword techniques "fundamental"[1] and other more difficult ones "advanced."[2]

I shall make it very clear that these styles do not represent the true Way of martial strategy, and thus I shall write down here what is good and evil, or right and wrong, in terms of martial strategy. My style, *Niten-Ichi-ryu*, is different in doctrine and method from others. Those commercial schools base their teaching on fancy techniques in order to attract and impress people and are not following the true Way.

Neither is it the right Way to limit one's learning to sword fighting. Such a person merely learns the basic body-shifting motions and how to swing a sword, and hopes thus to acquire techniques for winning in combat. One cannot learn the Way of victory with such a limited method.

Here, I will describe the shortcomings of other styles, which should help you appreciate and understand the principle of *Niten-Ichi-ryu*.

STYLES WHICH EMPHASIZE
A LONGER SWORD[3]

There are styles that seem to particularly enjoy using longer swords. According to the principle of my style, such methods are not authentic.

The reason for this is that those who are involved with these styles are caught up in the idea of the length of the sword, without knowing the true principle of victory over one's opponents. Such people intend to win against the opponent by fighting from a distance. They often say that each inch gives one an advantage, but in reality, those who believe in this know nothing about martial strategy. Therefore, if one attempts to win a battle by using a longer sword, believing that the longer sword makes a difference, it shows that he has a weak mind and is ignorant of the principle of martial strategy. I deem such a martial strategy inadequate and lacking authenticity.

Being rather unwieldy, the longer sword becomes very inconvenient if one wants to get close to one's opponent and grapple with him. In such a case, the longer sword simply becomes a burden, and a shorter sword would be superior to a longer one. Those who prefer the longer sword have their reasons, but they are not based on objective truth. If judged in the light of the truth of the Way, the advantage of a longer sword has no basis. Think about it: if one were forced to use a short sword rather than the preferred longer sword, would that necessarily mean that one would lose the battle?

It is not appropriate for a martial strategist to prefer using a longer sword when there is not enough space above, below, or to either side of the battle area. Also, wishing you had a longer sword when you are only equipped with a short sword is wrong. Such an undesirable attitude stems from the fact that you are not truly following the Way of martial strategy.

There are those who are not physically strong enough to use a longer sword. But it has been said that the greater includes the lesser, so it would be incorrect to blindly abhor a longer sword. It is the mental attitude that favors a longer sword that should be cautioned against. Metaphorically speaking, in warfare a short sword can be compared to a small army, while a longer sword to a large army. Is it not possible for a smaller force to defeat a larger one? There have been many cases whereby a smaller force defeated a larger force. In my *Niten-Ichi-ryu*, it is considered taboo to become bigoted and narrow-minded. Study this matter well.

HARD SWING OF SWORD IN OTHER STYLES

There should not be any particular distinction made between a hard and a gentle swing of the sword. If you try to wield your sword in a forceful manner, your movements will become rough, lacking precision. Being rough does not necessarily make you a winner.

A forceful, strong wielding of your sword is ineffective at cutting down a man. Even in a practice-cutting situation, it is not advisable for you to swing the sword with more than the necessary force.

No matter who your opponent is, you should not think of cutting him down either strongly or gently. At the moment you cut down your opponent, the only thing that you should be thinking of is wielding your sword with the intention of killing your opponent. Do not consciously focus on how strongly or gently you should swing your sword.

If you depend on swinging the sword hard, the results could be undesirable. If your sword hits your opponent's too hard, you could break it. So there should be no such thing as swinging the sword forcefully.

In warfare involving armies, if you attempt to gather a large group of strong soldiers to fight hard, the enemy will do the same. Without the principle and method behind it, you cannot win a battle.

In my martial strategy, one is taught not to attempt to use a method that is against the natural principle and that one should not use irrational techniques. One must learn how to win a battle in accordance with the principle of martial strategy. You should study this well.

THE USE OF THE SHORT
SWORD IN OTHER STYLES

It is not in accordance with the true method to win a combat by only using a short sword. Since olden times, a distinction has been made between *tachi* (long sword) and *katana* (sword) according to the difference in their lengths. A physically strong person has no problem wielding a longer sword, so they have no reason to choose a short sword. Referring purely to the length of a weapon, a physically stronger person should prefer weapons such as the spear and the halberd.

When using a short sword, you may get too caught up in the idea of cutting your opponent down by taking advantage of an opening as your opponent swings his longer sword. Someone who uses the short sword may also keep thinking of jumping into the opponent to cut him or to get close enough to grapple him. This tendency to get caught up in the length of the sword is not a good one. By using the short sword, one may become too passive, just waiting for an opening and not being forceful enough to make a decisive movement, which is wrong.

It should also be observed that it is not a good idea to wield the short sword when you have many opponents at once. Someone who has trained in the use of the short sword may try to cut through his opponents, jumping up and running about. But all this effort may be in vain, and he may become confused if he is forced to be constantly on the defensive. This is not in accordance with the principle of martial strategy.

If you engage in combat, you should keep your mind and body straight and strong. It is important that you should chase your opponent(s) and make them jump up and down so that they become confused and unstable. The same thing can be said of warfare involving armies. If the time comes when you get involved in a large-scale battle, you may as well bring a large and strong army with which to destroy the enemy as quickly and completely as possible.

People often emphasize the techniques of blocking, parrying, dodging, and ducking in their daily training in martial strategy. These are all based on a passive attitude, which makes them act in the same passive manner during actual combat situations and gives their opponents the chance to become dominant. The Way of martial strategy is straight in its form and based on the truth. According to the principle of martial strategy, you must be able to control your opponent(s) at all times. Study this point well.

VARIETIES OF SWORD TECHNIQUES IN OTHER STYLES

There are those who try to impress beginners by demonstrating many different techniques in the art of sword fighting. This amounts to commercialization of the Way of martial strategy, which is not desirable conduct in the world of martial strategy.

To begin with, it is wrong to believe that there are different ways of cutting an opponent in a combat situation. There should not be any difference in one's way of using a sword regardless of one's opponent. Whether one is familiar with martial strategy or not, whether one is a woman or a child, the methods are all the same in striking, hitting, and cutting down. Slight exceptions are thrusting and side-wielding techniques.

The most important fact to remember is that my martial strategy is a method of killing an opponent, and there can only be so many ways of doing that. However, depending on the circumstance, such as obstacles in the combat area, it becomes inconvenient to use the sword in the same manner all the time. For this reason, there are five basic methods of using the sword as described previously.

Apart from the five basic methods of holding the sword, twisting the hands in cutting techniques, bending the body, and jumping over to the side to cut the opponent are not in accordance with the principle of martial strategy. In order to cut an opponent, it is not effective to twist, bend, or jump to the side to cut one's opponent. They are all useless methods.

In my martial strategy, it is crucial that one should face an opponent with a direct and strong attitude. By using the principle of martial strategy, one should confuse and disarray the opponent, thus defeating him. You must study this hard.

AN EMPHASIS ON SPECIFIC WAYS OF
HOLDING A SWORD IN OTHER STYLES

It is wrong to place an emphasis on specific ways of holding a sword as the subject of primary importance. It is possible to assume a stance with your sword when there is no actual opponent in front of you. It is not correct to specify a rigid pattern by claiming that a certain method is based on old precedents or else is a new way of doing things. In the world of martial arts there should be no such thing as a rigid pattern. In martial strategy, you must use the techniques which would most intimidate your opponent. When the word "position" is used, it implies that things are static or rigid in form. For example, if we say that one established a castle or settled down at an army headquarters, it usually means that the castle and the headquarters are immovable because of their established, rigid form. However, in the world of martial strategy, it is imperative that one should take the initiative in combat situations at all times in order to control one's opponent. You must study this well.

The Way of martial strategy is based on the idea of defeating your opponent by taking advantage of your opponent's mental weakness. This state of mind could have been caused by confusion, anger, surprise, or threats that have been initiated by you. So it is not in accordance with the principle of martial strategy to let your opponent take the initiative during combat by conforming to a certain posture or stance for form's sake. In my martial strategy, therefore, it is said that one can take a specific posture without emphasizing it (with no specific attention to the form itself). You must avoid becoming passive or too defensive by concentrating on the idea of forming a "position."

Even in a warfare involving armies, it is essential that you face the battle fully knowing your own strength as well as that of the enemy. You must be informed about the size of your enemy and the condition of the battlefield as well as the degree of morale of your own army. Before battle begins, you must have judged the advantages and disadvantages that your army has over the enemy.

There is a tremendous difference in advantage between you taking the initiative to attack and your opponent making the first move. Even when you intend to take a good position holding the sword and deal with your opponent's attack successfully by blocking and parrying, as long as you keep assuming a defensive form, you might as well be swinging a spear or a halberd over a fence. At the moment when you face your opponent, your spirit and energy must be so sure that you would even pull up a fence picket and use it against your opponent in place of a spear or halberd. You must have that much fighting spirit and energy. Study this very well.

EYE FOCUS IN OTHER STYLES

Depending on the style, people are taught to focus their eyes on their opponent's sword, hands, face, or feet during combat. If you make a deliberate effort to focus your eyes on a particular point, it will distract your concentration and become detrimental to the Way of martial strategy. Take a kickball player,[4] for example. He does not focus his eyes purposely on the ball itself, but freely kicks it when it comes close to him. He also chases the ball without directing his eyes on it at all times. He can kick the ball all over in different ways, which is the result of training and experience.

There are also those who can stand a fan on their nose or juggle several swords with no difficulty as if they were balls. They do not fix their eyes on the objects when performing such feats. They see the objects naturally without actually having to focus on them. This becomes possible as the result of training and experience.

Similarly, in the Way of martial strategy, once you have engaged in actual battles and mastered the principles of fighting, you will be able to see the distance and speed of your opponent's sword as well as other things important to victory in combat. In essence, the eyes must be focused on the opponent's mind in martial strategy, on the inner self. Even in a battle involving armies, one should focus on the total condition of the enemy and not on any particular point.

Of the two methods of seeing, *kan* and *ken*, use *kan* to detect the enemy's condition and to maintain a sense of perspective in order to perceive the rhythm-timing of the battle. Whether the battle is going in your favor or not, once you clearly perceive the overall situation using *kan*, you will lead your army to victory. It is, therefore, of primary importance to use *kan* as the method of seeing.

Both in army warfare and one-to-one combat, you should not concentrate your eyes on one particular point. As it was earlier explained, if you try to pay too much attention to the details, you will lose a sense of perspective of the overall situation. In this way, you may lose control of yourself and then you will also lose the battle. You must understand this principle well and study it hard.

FOOTWORK IN OTHER STYLES

Many different kinds of unnaturally fast footwork are taught, such as "floating foot," "jumping foot," "springing-up foot," "stomping foot," and "crow's foot." Not all of these are correct according to the principle of my martial strategy.

Regarding the "floating foot," it is not good to teach such footwork, because there is an undesirable tendency to have feet float during combat to begin with. You must have stable footwork in a combat situation and do not need the "floating foot." As for the "jumping foot," your stance becomes rigid and legs become tight at the moment of landing. It is not possible to jump many times in sequence, so it is wrong to adopt such footwork.

As for the "springing-up foot," one cannot fight efficiently if he intends constantly to spring up. The "stomping foot" makes one too defensive, and this is particularly undesirable.

There are other types of footwork, such as the "crow's foot," characterized by quick, small steps, which are unnaturally fast. When engaging in combat, you may have to encounter your opponents in swamps, deep rice fields, valleys and streams, fields full of stones, and narrow pathways. This would make it impossible to use the unnatural, quick types of footwork, let alone the "jumping" footwork.

In my martial strategy, the same footwork is used for walking ordinarily in the street as for combat situations. Depending on your opponent's movements, you must move your feet in such a way that you efficiently keep your balance and control at all times, whether you are moving fast or slowly.

Proper footwork is also important in army warfare. It becomes difficult to defeat the enemy if you move too fast without knowing the enemy's tactics. If you walk too slowly, you may miss the opportunity to gain victory by lunging at the enemy as they give you an opening when they appear sluggish. When the enemy becomes unsettled—lacking in harmony and stability—you must attack them at once. Gain victory at once without giving your enemy the opportunity to recover their strength. Study this well.

MATTERS OF SPEED IN OTHER STYLES

In the world of martial strategy, you should not place particular emphasis on speed. Things are fast or slow in relationship to the rhythm-timing of each situation—it is all relative. Those who excel in any particular field do not appear or strive to be fast.

For example, there are professional couriers with great running skill who cover many, many miles a day. But this does not mean that they run fast all day and night. An inexperienced runner may not even be able to cover a similar distance with an entire day's effort.

In the field of No[5] dance, if a novice singer tries to follow an accomplished one, the former feels as if he is behind the rhythm and has to get busier. For an inexperienced drummer, even such quiet and slow music as *Oi-matsu*[6] would be too fast and he would feel uncomfortable playing it. One should not beat the drum too fast in music such as *Takasago*[7] either, even though it is supposed to have a swift tempo.

It is often said that he who hurries tumbles. This means that one should not sacrifice a proper rhythm-timing for the sake of mere speed.

Needless to say, being too slow is just as bad. An accomplished person performs without apparent effort, and yet is in harmony with the necessary rhythm. In any field, a person with experience and skill does not seem to be in a hurry during a performance. You may be able to understand the principle from these examples.

Especially in the Way of martial strategy, speed alone is not good. If you have to confront your opponents in swamps or deep rice fields, you will not be able to maneuver your body and feet very quickly. As for your sword, if you try to swing it with an emphasis on speed, you may find that the sword does not cut well, as the long sword is not the same as a fan or a short sword. Try to understand this point well.

In army warfare, it is not good to be hasty either. You do not need to worry about being slow as long as you adopt the principle of "pressing down the pillow." Also, when the enemy comes after you aggressively with reckless speed, you must react calmly and maintain your own pace. This is called *somuku* ("disregard"), which means that you should resist the temptation to be affected by your opponent's pace. You must study well the psychological aspects of martial strategy shown in these examples.

BASIC AND ADVANCED TECHNIQUES IN OTHER STYLES

How can one describe techniques in the world of martial strategy as basic or advanced? In some arts and certain other fields, there may be special knowledge that needs to be transmitted in secret. In such a case, it may be proper to start from the basics and gradually move to the advanced step by step. However, as far as fighting strategy is concerned, it is absurd to say that one should fight an opponent either with basic techniques or with advanced techniques.

In my martial strategy, I let the beginner learn the techniques he can most easily absorb. Then as he makes progress, I guide him, in gradual manner, into understanding the more profound aspects of the principle.

Generally speaking, however, I try to teach techniques that have a basis in practical experience, so there is no need to distinguish between basic techniques and advanced ones. Just imagine that you are trying to get to a point deep in the mountains and you keep going deeper and deeper. You are bound eventually to find yourself on the other side of the mountains. In every field and art, there are both occasions when very advanced techniques have to be used and times when we can easily get by using only basic techniques.

How can you talk about what should be kept a secret and what shouldn't in the world of martial strategy? In my martial strategy, I detest the use of written pledges by students and penalties against those who break the rules and regulations. Judging properly each student's natural ability and potential, I try to teach them the correct Way of martial strategy by dispelling any erroneous notions they may have about it. The purpose of my martial strategy is to teach my students the true Way of the samurai and help them gain confidence. Train well in this Way.

EPILOGUE

In this volume, I have described certain aspects of other styles in nine different sections. It might have been clearer if I had written about each style in detail with descriptions of their basic and advanced techniques. But I deliberately avoided mentioning the names of the styles I was referring to, because each style has a different view of each technique and there are many ways to interpret and execute them, depending on the individual. As time goes on, there is an inevitable change in interpretation and execution of each technique even within the same style. Therefore, I thought it would be wise not to mention the styles by name lest there be confusion in the future.

I have described the general characteristics of other styles in nine different sections. Judging from the viewpoint of the common sense of society, those styles are all distorted, insisting on a longer or a shorter sword, a forceful or gentle way of swinging it, a general or detailed view of strategy. They are all one-sided. It is probably clear to all, without my mentioning any names, which techniques belong to which styles.

In my *Niten-Ichi-ryu*, there are no basic or advanced techniques in sword usage. There is no special teaching or secret related to the positions of holding the sword. The only important thing is that one sincerely pursues the Way of martial strategy in order to attain its principle.

To: Terao Magonojo

May 12, 1645
Shin-men Musashi

ANALYSIS

I n this volume, Musashi concentrates on criticism of other styles and schools of martial strategy. He compares them with his own system *Niten-Ichi-ryu*. A severe criticism is given to other styles that claim that a beginner should learn certain techniques designed for a beginner while an advanced practitioner should be taught other, more difficult techniques. He feels there should not be any such differentiation of techniques. As Musashi's view is based on the simple and direct philosophy that the only purpose of learning how to use the sword is to defeat the opponent in combat, then how can one differentiate between techniques for the beginner and those for the advanced student?

However, Musashi concedes that a beginner should be introduced to techniques he can most easily absorb and that this should vary according to the individual involved. Thus, he insists it is not the technique that should be altered but rather the student who should be differentiated according to his or her natural ability and aptitudes. If there is something that a beginner has difficulty understanding, let him wait to learn it at a later time.

Every person has different strengths and weaknesses, so one beginner may find a particular technique easy while another may find it impossible to learn at first. This is the reason why Musashi did not create a rigid order in which the techniques must be taught to the students. A person should be taught whatever he can learn and absorb, he maintains. Although he named his style or method *Niten-Ichi-ryu*, it seems that he was really against any "systematized" method. His main purpose was not to propagate *Niten-Ichi-ryu* but to teach whoever wished to learn how to use the sword to win. The only condition that Musashi placed on his potential students was that they be ready to learn not only how to use the sword but also how to kill the opponent in combat. Musashi was not interested in teaching his students just how to manipulate the sword, which anyone could have taught. His constant interest was to teach his students how to be winners.

Under normal circumstances, when we discuss the strength of a particular style we are referring to its size in terms of the number of students as well as its sphere of influence. So an interesting question arises regarding Musashi's *Niten-Ichi-ryu*, which does not have a large number of disciples, unlike *Itto-ryu* ("One-Sword style") or *Shinkage-ryu* ("New-Shadow style"). There is a small number of people who still practice *Niten-Ichi-ryu* in the Kyusyu area, but *Itto-ryu* has survived for centuries and has become the most important basis for modern kendo. So what has prevented Musashi's style from becoming as popular?

It has been mentioned already that Musashi's method of teaching was individualistically oriented, varying according to each person's ability.[9] He taught without any rigid order of learning. Students from other styles or schools learn from a systematized curriculum and perform techniques according to their step-by-step teaching. Under such conditions, good students are easy to spot, for they are the ones who follow the given subject well.

However, in *Niten-Ichi-ryu*, it is opposite in the sense that good students should not conform to any particular method of fighting, they simply must win at all times. Winning, never losing at all, is the standard of proficiency for students who adhere to *Niten-Ichi-ryu*. It is ironic that the emphasis on absolute strength in combat which characterizes *Niten-Ichi-ryu* has resulted in its "weakness" as a systematized style. It is obvious that determining the true proficiency of the student in *Niten-Ichi-ryu* is a difficult task. The student in this school must fight to prove that he is good. He has to continuously fight until he can say that he could be called a true student of *Niten-Ichi-ryu* by virtue of the fact that he has defeated a certain number of opponents. If one carries this theory to an extreme degree, there is a certain weakness in it. One could become the best student of *Niten-Ichi-ryu* by defeating all "available" opponents, but perhaps these are not the worthiest opponents.

Musashi writes that if your secret techniques are so important that you want to protect them from others then they are probably not that valuable for anyone. In order to point out the absurdity of so-called "profound" techniques in other styles, Musashi argues that if one goes deep into the mountains he will eventually come out on the other side, which is the "beginning" of the mountains from a different side. Similarly, there are no secret techniques in martial strategy. Depending on the situation, one uses different techniques, whether complicated or simple, in order to defend oneself and defeat the opponent.

Many other styles or schools, as Musashi observes, purposely set up a system that includes various techniques of different levels with the ultimate learning of "secret" or "the most profound" techniques, in order to ensure perpetuation of their existence. In other words, their existence depends on these "mysterious, secret" techniques that their students are conditioned to seek as the ultimate. No wonder then that they are eager to protect them from others at any cost. In *Niten-Ichi-ryu* there is nothing secret to hide. The only strict and outstanding tenet would be "one must be able to defeat others at any cost," which is so abstract that it cannot be imitated by others.

Because of his realization of the importance of each individual's different ability, Musashi believed that it would be right to adopt an appropriate method of teaching for each person. Musashi's approach seems to be ideal as far as true education is concerned: it brings out the greatest amount of potential from each student.

Musashi's solitary life might have made him believe that the only dependable person in the world was himself. In order to assert his existence and to assure his position in the world, he must have developed himself to be the most worthy human being that he could be. However, Musashi was not a blind individualist. He recognized that other people are in the same predicament, whether they know it or not, and that is the reason why his teaching method is so individualistically oriented. Here one should be reminded of the sentences written at the beginning of the book: "I have had no teacher in whatever I have studied or engaged in."

One of Musashi's harshest criticisms of other styles is directed to their insistence on a particular length of sword—long versus short. He is critical of both ways, claiming that it is not a correct attitude in martial strategy to depend on any special length of the weapon. Regarding the schools that specialize in usage of the longer sword, Musashi observes that if you concentrate only on the length of the sword itself, you cannot concentrate on the opponent, and that the only purpose of martial strategy is to defeat or kill the opponent. In other words, Musashi warns that your mind should be occupied only by the purpose of combat, which is to become a winner, and for that the length of the sword is irrelevant.

As for the short sword, Musashi criticizes it by pointing out that a devotion to this weapon alone distorts the warrior's mind. If one holds the short sword, he has to look at all times for an opening in the opponent's defense in order to step inside the normal fighting range and use the short sword. According to Musashi, this idea of constantly trying to shorten the distance between oneself and the opponent is not based on a correct notion of martial strategy. The crucial thing is that one should not be attached to any one particular size or shape of weapon. The person who uses the weapon is the subject and the weapon is the secondary object. Those who depend on shape or size in a weapon are already demonstrating their mental weakness, because they have forgotten the fact that it is they who are facing the opponent, not the weapon. The weapon does not move by itself, it is the person who must use it.

Musashi's famous fight against Sasaki Kojiro has already been referred to, but now would be an appropriate time to expand on the legendary meeting between the two great warriors in 1612. According to *Niten-ki*, Kojiro was known for his exceptionally long sword, which was nicknamed the "laundry pole." He had thus far defeated every challenger and was the instructor of the Hosokawa family when Musashi finally confronted this extraordinary samurai. Musashi's genius enabled him to perceive that Kojiro's strength lay in his manipulation of the long sword rather than his actual technique in the art of sword fighting in the authentic sense. This point is crucial, for Musashi was able to demonstrate his martial strategy to be superior. He clearly demonstrated in this combat against Kojiro that he was able to engage in combat under any condition and defeat any opponent. Despite his great skill and strength in sword fighting, Kojiro was too occupied with the weapon itself. Musashi took advantage of Kojiro's psychological weakness by using a long wooden sword made out of an old oar. Kojiro must have been surprised to see the long wooden sword that Musashi carried on his shoulder. Until then, every opponent had used shorter swords than Kojiro's. Kojiro's attention was focussed on Musashi's sword itself, especially its length, and this made his martial strategy less flexible and less effective. The historic combat lasted only a short time. Musashi's sword struck Kojiro's head and in a sense Kojiro became the victim of his own long weapon, which had defeated so many previous opponents.

As far as the use of power in wielding the sword, Musashi suggests that it should be neither too light nor too great. If you swing the sword either too hard or too gently, it will not cut. Musashi is also critical of those who try to impress others by the number of techniques they know rather than their quality. In any field, basic knowledge is important. Practicing fancy techniques which lack substance can be compared to the creation of a building that has a beautiful ornament on top but which rests on a weak foundation. Not only is this meaningless, but it is also dangerous.

Eye focus and posture are also very important in the art of sword fighting. Although many schools insist on one particular method, Musashi does not stray from the principle of his martial strategy. Some schools maintain that one should always focus on the opponent's eyes, while others insist that it should be on the opponent's hands as they control the sword. Still others teach that the best spot to focus on during combat is the opponent's feet. Musashi feels that they are not all wrong in that any one of those techniques can be effective at a certain time and a certain situation.

However, it is wrong, according to Musashi, to focus on only one thing. If one's eyes are directed on a single spot, the mind will also be limited, not reaching its full potential. The mind must be free and flowing all over the fighting range so that it can control and dominate the opponent. Musashi uses the example of a then-popular ball game—an expert kickball player does not actually look at the ball itself and manages never to lose the ball. Similarly, an acrobat does not fix his eyes on the wire as he crosses over it.

Regarding speed, Musashi points out that being fast is not necessarily a good thing in martial strategy. It goes without saying that being slow is not always good, either. A true expert in any art moves in a seemingly gentle and slow way, yet with total concentration, leaving no room for error. One should never try to accomplish any task too quickly and risk neglecting some essential aspect. There is such a thing as absolute speed which transcends the normal concept of fast and slow. (An example of it is the earth's rotation, which we do not feel.) There is no dualistic idea of slow and fast movements in absolute movement. Musashi seems to refer to the same concept when he discusses the matter of speed.

So it seems clear why Musashi's method does not suit everyone. His way of instruction is more effective in a one-to-one rather than a group instruction situation. Musashi's fighting strategy stresses the individual from the beginning to the end. It may be safely said that he was always more interested in teaching one exceptional student who had the potential of understanding the ultimate technique than one hundred mediocre students. It may also be correct to suppose that Musashi's true strength was so hidden within himself that it could not be taught to others.

In this volume, Musashi points to the lack of fundamental spirit in other styles and schools. His method was directed toward creating an individual with a strong, independent spirit who would be able to live in the world as a winner in any adverse situation. In Musashi's eyes, other styles were more about purely physical techniques which held no substance. Their students would become knowledgeable but not truly strong, assertive human beings with a burning desire for self-actualization and survival.

VOLUME FIVE **KŪ**

TRANSLATION

I am now about to describe the principle of my martial strategy of *Niten-Ichi-ryu* in this volume, *Kū*.[1] *Kū* is the realm of matters beyond ordinary human understanding. One must be enlightened as to what truly exists in order to know what does not exist. When one is incapable of understanding something it should not be called *Kū*. This is simply ignorance.

In the world of martial strategy, one who is not thoroughly familiar with the way of the samurai will not come to know the meaning of *Kū*; he will instead be disarrayed and confused. When a person faces a deadlock in life, with no way out, he often refers to this condition as *Kū*, which is incorrect.

For a samurai, the true understanding of *Kū* can be attained in the thorough practice of the Way of martial strategy. He learns various martial arts, and also becomes fully aware of his duty as a samurai in daily life. His mind should be devoid of delusion and he should be constantly disciplining himself in both body and mind. He should also try to cultivate the two methods of seeing: *kan* and *ken*. Using these methods, he must become able to observe and judge things correctly. His true *Kū* is found where there is no cloud of delusion and when he is free from a world of bewilderment in life.

As long as one is not enlightened about the Way of truth, one might believe that one's own Way is correct, whether it be the Way of Buddha or other worldly matters. It could happen, however, that his

Way will not be in accordance with the truth if judged in the light of the true doctrine of the world. It is possible to unconsciously ignore the true Way simply by being self-centered or prejudiced. One must understand this point well.

As you pursue the Way of the truth, try to maintain a straight and sincere attitude based on the serious intentions of applying the Way of martial strategy to daily living. This becomes possible as you grasp the true meaning of martial strategy and its principle from a greater perspective. With a correct and clear understanding of the principle of martial strategy, you will be able to view the world of *Kū* as a guide to enlightenment.

In the world of *Kū*, there is no evil, only good prevails. Knowledge and skill in the human world have limitations, as does the principle of martial strategy. However, mind and spirit belong to *Kū*, which is boundless.

To: Terao Magonojo   May 12, 1645
                                                Shin-men Musashi

ANALYSIS

Musashi does not write about combat strategy in this final volume, *Kū*, which translated literally means "sky," "emptiness," "nothingness," and "void." Musashi's concept of *Kū* does not include any negative meaning, and therefore, it seems appropriate to express it with such words as "boundlessness," "infinity," "the ultimate," and "limitlessness." In the realm of *Kū*, there does not exist any dualistic tension—there is no enemy or friend, no rich or poor, no life or death. It is no wonder, then, that Musashi does not refer to fighting strategy in *Kū*, where the self and others become one, the self and nature are one, and all things are in "oneness," in harmony and peace.

In a concrete sense, *Kū* is the domain of an enlightened individual who has reached the highest stage of his art. There occurs a certain miracle in the world of *Kū*—differentiation and equality become the same thing. In other words, everything is different and discriminated, and at the same time everything is the same and equal.

Musashi, who had consistently maintained the most pragmatic approach to martial strategy by insisting that the purpose of training in sword fighting was to win in combat, has now come to translate the knowledge and techniques of martial strategy onto a higher plain—spirituality. In Zen this is the point at which one acquires satori (enlightenment) and comes to know the meaning of existence as well as nonexistence, leaving all doubts and questions behind. This is the world of newness, or to put it another way, this is the original world which one comes to see with pure knowledge and without conceptualization.

The fact that Musashi had experienced more than sixty life-and-death battles makes his spirituality truly authentic—it is not merely talk and definitely not escapism. His world of *Kū* is where total peacefulness prevails—there is no killing or fighting among people there. Musashi must have come to realize the absurdity of wielding the sword just for the sake of proving his physical strength and skill.[2] When used by an enlightened individual, the sword helps others live and prosper rather than cause death and destruction.

The world of *Kū* is where one can truly know and feel what exists and what doesn't. One knows and understands all and yet is not attached to knowledge. One is not even attached to oneself, therefore he is free in the truest sense of the word. In the world of *Kū*, one becomes harmonious with the universe to the extent that the self feels at one with it. According to Musashi, the realm of *Kū* can be reached through a complete understanding and absorption of the Way of martial strategy. One's state of mind in the world of *Kū* is like a shiny blue sky which has no clouds—free from doubt and confusion.

Musashi teaches that one must be faithful to the Way of the truth by affirming the True Self, which is the original nature of the self before it comes to have knowledge of evil. The True Self is *Mu*[3] ("void" or "emptiness") and it resides in the world of *Kū*. It seeks harmony and peace among people and detests conflicts and confrontation. It seems that Musashi's state of mind toward the end of his life truly reflects this peaceful, serene atmosphere. He was like an enlightened Zen practitioner who comes to the marketplace to mingle with others without any pretense. People around do not know who he is. They only know that he is gentle, cordial, and compassionate. Only in an emergency does he suddenly and spontaneously demonstrate his incredible power.

There seem to be two main reasons for a samurai to seek this world of *Kū*. A samurai's duty was to train in the art of sword fighting and serve his lord using his skill of fighting, either in one-to-one combat or in warfare involving armies. No matter how one looks at it, a samurai had to face the imminent possibility of death at all times. In order to attain inner peace and come to terms with the fear and anguish of death, he must have searched the world of *Kū*, where only peace and harmony prevail. From a psychological viewpoint, a samurai's strong desire to attain *Kū* is natural given his life's predicament. No one wishes to die and everyone fears death, but for a samurai death is constantly present. In seeking out the realm of *Kū*, a samurai was trying not to escape from death itself, but rather to find a way to deal with the fear of death.

Another important reason for a samurai to seek the world of *Kū* was to gain absolute confidence that he would be victorious at any time and in any combat situation. A samurai's desire to win and survive made him train himself physically and mentally beyond imagination. The ultimate levels of physical skill, mental discipline, and spiritual enlightenment are all results of hard and constant practice. A serious samurai's effort was rewarded with the discovery and creation of the new world of *Kū*, where he realized the meaning of the true sword . . . to help others and live with others in harmony, and not to kill and destroy others. Wisdom in *Kū* is based on peace within the self and with others.

NOTES

pp. 2–7   WINNING AND SUCCESS

1. *The Book of Five Rings*...Musashi explains his total philosophy of martial strategy in terms of the belief that the Universe consists of Earth, Water, Fire, Wind, and *Kū*. *Kū* connotes emptiness or nothingness, and it embraces the remaining four elements. The five elements, each of which on its own is a complete circle, are connected with each other in such a way that they compose a greater, total circle as well. As for the meaning behind the term "ring" itself, it connotes an endless circle with no beginning and no end. This concept is diametrically opposed to the dualistic Western idea of life and death, for in the Buddhist philosophy of life and death, there is no beginning and no ending. The ring is perfect as well as endless, and a perfect living being is endless in its existence. Other meanings of the "five rings" include:

    a. Five circular things, referring to the human elbows, knees, and head.

    b. In the human body, according to Japanese tradition, the knees are called the "ring of earth," the navel is called the "ring of water," the chest is referred to as the "ring of fire," the face is called the "ring of wind," and the top of the head is referred to as the "ring of kū."

2. *sen*...This word also appears on pp. 11, 13, 94, 95, 98, 99, 101, 102, 111, 112. Also, refer to footnote on p. 152.

3. *utsuraseru*...This word also appears on pp. 102, 112, 113.

4. *kan* and *ken*...These words also appear on pp. 6, 65, 84, 85, 127, 128, 143. See footnote p. 152

5. *dojo*...This word also appears on p. 36, and footnote on p. 150.

pp. 9-17   A BIOGRAPHICAL SKETCH OF
                MIYAMOTO MUSASHI

1. a samurai...See footnote on p. 150.

2. Arima Kihei...See pp. 33 and 48. see #1 on Map p. 156

3. *Shinto-ryu*...See footnote on p. 150.

4. Akiyama...See pp. 33 and 48. see #2 on Map p. 156

5. Kyoto...See footnote on p. 150. see #5 on Map p. 156

6. Yoshioka family...See footnote on p. 151. see #5 on Map p. 156

7. Shishido Baiken...See footnote on p. 151. see #7 on Map p. 156

8. Sasaki Kojiro...This name appears on pp. 50, 113, 136 and footnote on p. 154. see #9 on Map p. 156

9. *Niten-ki*...See footnote on p. 151.

10. Kumamoto...see #12 on Map p. 156

pp. 18-27   MIND OF SAMURAI

1. *Hyogo*...See footnote on p. 143.

2. *Tsukahara Bokuden*...See color insert #7

THE BOOK OF FIVE RINGS

pp. 33-59   VOLUME ONE **EARTH**

1. Kan-ei Era (1624–1643)...Musashi started to write *The Book of Five Rings* in October 1643.

2. Province of Higo (presently Kumamoto prefecture)...Located in the west central part of Kyushu Island. see Map p. 156

3. Kyushu...Japan consists of four main islands, Hokkaido, Honshu, Shikoku and Kyushu.

4. *Kan-non*...The goddess of mercy, who is endowed with unlimited compassion, patience, and mercy. She sits at the left side of Buddha.

5. a samurai...The samurai served the shogun and was trained in literature and the martial arts as well as military tactics. The samurai occupied the highest position of the social caste system, which consisted of samurais, farmers, artisans, and merchants. The samurai class rose to prominence in Japanese society at the time of Minamoto Yoritomo's establishment of *Kamakura Bakufu* (Shogunke Government) in 1192.

6. Province of Harima...Once located in the western part of Honshu Island. Today the area is part of Okayama and Hyogo prefecture. see Map p. 156

7. *Shinto-ryu*...It is a name of style of the art of sword fighting. It is said that there have been more than two hundred styles in the art of sword-fighting in Japanese history.

8. Kyoto...Located in the western part of Honshu Island. It is surrounded by such prefectures as Hyogo, Fukui, Nara, Osaka, and Shiga.

9. Kashima and Katori shrines...Historically, having produced many renowned warriors, the Kashima and Katori shrines are famous for traditional martial arts instructions called *Kashima Shinto-ryu* and *Katori Shinto-ryu*, respectively.

10. Province of Hitachi (presently Ibaraki and Chiba prefectures)...Located in the east central part of Kyushu Island, slightly northeast of Edo (Tokyo). Today, the Kashima Shrine is located in the Ibaraki prefecture and the Katori Shrine is in Chiba prefecture.

11. dojo...Literally translated, it is "the place of the way." It refers to a school or training hall of martial arts as well as Zen.

12. *sake*...Japanese rice wine.

13. Fujiwara family...A noble family with powerful political influence, the Fujiwaras held the reins of government from the end of the tenth to the beginning of the eleventh century. Fujiwara Kamatari (614–669) laid its foundation of power. The most famous of all Fujiwara was Michinaga (966–1027).

14. Musashi refers here to a concept that is often addressed in Japan, *"Tekizai-Tekisho,"* which can be literally translated as "the right

material to the right place."

15. According to the concept in Buddhism, all things in the Universe consist of these five elements.

16. *Kū*...See footnote on p. 141 and p. 147.

17. *Hyoshi*...It is a difficult word to translate into English. It connotes such concepts as "timing," "rhythm" and "tempo." In this book, I use the word "rhythm-timing" to describe it.

18. It is interesting to compare these nine articles of Musashi's teaching with Buddha's eight teachings, which are: (1) The correct observation of things and matters. (2) Correct reasoning. (3) Usage of the correct language. (4) Correct conduct. (5) Correct concentration and stability of mind. (6) Correct effort toward one's objectives. (7) Correct thought and selflessness. (8) Correct living.

19. Einstein wrote a letter to one of his friends, who had just lost a daughter. In the letter, trying to console the friend in pain, he mentioned that he felt a certain humility as a finite being in the universe.

20. *Niten-ki* ("The Chronicle of Two Heavens")...Written in 1755, it is an unofficial biography of Musashi by Toyota Matashiro, his son, Hikojiro, and his grandson, Sakon-e-mon. As a biography of Musashi, it is one of the most systematized, although, due to the fact that it was written about one hundred years after Musashi's death, we may not depend on it for complete accuracy.

21. For example, Yamada Jirokichi, author of a history of Japanese Kendo, does not include Musashi among the foremost sword fighters in Japanese history. Also, writers such as Naoki Sanjugo and Sakaguchi Ango are skeptical of Musashi's true ability as a sword fighter.

22. Yagyu Tajima no Kami Munenori (1571–1646)...He was a retainer to Shogun Iemitsu (the third Tokugawa shogun) as instructor in charge of martial arts, *ken-jitsu* in particular. He is also the author of the book called *Hyohokadensho* ("Message from a Strategist").

23. Ono Jiro-e-mon Tada-aki (1565–1629)...He was the second successor to Ito-Ittosai, founder of *Itto-ryu*. Tada-aki was also called Ten-zen and served the second shogun, Hidetada, as instructor in charge of martial arts, *ken-jitsu* in particular.

24. Shishido Baiken...After defeating the Yoshioka family in Kyoto, Musashi met Shishido Baiken in Mi-e prefecture. see #7 on Map p. 156

25. Yoshioka family...This family was known as the most outstanding practitioners of martial strategy in Kyoto. Yoshioka Shoza-e-mon Kempo served Shogun Ashikaga Yoshiaki as instructor in charge of martial strategy. Yoshioka Seijuro and Denshichiro, who fought and were defeated by Musashi, were his sons. Musashi's challenge to the Yoshioka family took place, according to *Niten-ki*, in 1604. see #5 on Map p. 156

pp. 63-86   VOLUME TWO **WATER**

1. It is noteworthy that Musashi, in the middle of the Japanese feudal age, speaks of a concept of equality among people, although it is not of the same kind as that of democracy.

2. The Japanese word *kamae*, means "posture," "stance," or "position."

3. The "Way" connotes the "art"; in this case, Musashi refers to knowing the true essence of the art of swordsmanship.

4. It is called *jo-dan* in Japanese, literally "upper level."

5. It is called *ge-dan* in Japanese, literally "lower level."

6. It is called *hidari no waki* in Japanese, literally "left side."

7. It is called *migi no waki* in Japanese, literally "right side."

8. It is called *munen muso no uchi* in Japanese.

9. It is also known as a short-armed monkey.

10. Both *katsu* and *totsu* are phonetic expressions of shouting sounds used in fighting.

11. Musashi demonstrated this method when he fought an army of samurais from the Yoshioka family.

12. This tendency of exaggeration or mystification of the origins of various styles started to disappear as the samurais in general became better educated and more sophisticated.

pp. 91-117   VOLUME THREE **FIRE**

1. The word *sen* denotes "ahead," "superior," "precede," and other similar words. *Sensei* is someone who gives guidance to others,

such as a schoolteacher, an instructor in arts and sports, or whomever one wishes to address with respect, such as doctors and others with high social positions. *Sensei* appears on pp. 18, 19 and 20.

2. *"Tai"* in *tai no sen* and *"tai"* in *tai tai no sen* are different in meaning, the former denoting "to wait," the latter "to oppose."

3. A pillow used to be made of wood, and each person owned his or her own pillow suitable to his or her head. Thus, a pillow and a head used to be more closely related in thought in olden days in Japan.

4. Here Musashi refers to the importance of *kan*.

5. Compare it with another similar teaching called *soko o nuku* ("breaking through the bottom")—see pp. 101–102 and p. 111.

6. One can appreciate Musashi's keen perception of human nature and his application of psychology to martial strategy in this teaching of "catching."

7. It is called *sankai no kawari,* which literally means "change of mountains to sea," referring to Musashi's teaching that one should change techniques completely when they don't work. *San* in *sankai* means a "mountain," while *kai* means "sea." The same phonetic sounds are found in the number "3," which is also pronounced *"san,"* and in the meaning of "repetition," which is pronounced as *"kai."* Therefore, phonetically, "a mountain and sea" and "three times" are the same in Japanese, which Musashi cleverly uses in his writing for the double meaning.

8. *Soto-Goshu*...Literally it denotes "rat's head, horse's neck." The character representing *"Go"* in *"Goshu"* is 午 and not 牛. 午 represents a horse and 牛 a cow (ox).

9. This concept can be applied to many different situations which are unrelated to fighting or competing. For example, if you live in a foreign country without having sufficient command of the language of the country, you may come to feel less secure and even lose self-confidence. But, when you come to think of it, the native people are feeling somewhat the same feeling about you because they don't know about the country you come from. In such a case, you must take advantage of your knowledge about your own country. You may not know their language well, but you know your own language better than they do. Take advantage of your superior knowledge about yourself, and as time goes on,

you come to know their language and culture well enough to become comfortable, too.

pp. 121-138 VOLUME FOUR **WIND**

1. *Omote* is an entrance, and in this case means "fundamental" techniques.

2. *Oku* denotes "the interior," "inner parts," or "the depths." In this case, it means "advanced" or "secret teaching."

3. Musashi's most famous combat was against Sasaki Kojiro who specialized in using a sword longer than anyone's. Musashi defeated Kojiro by using a weapon longer than Kojiro's, thus proving that it was not correct to be attached only to a certain length of a sword. In other words, Musashi faced Kojiro's "strength" and turned it to his "weakness."

4. a kickball player...The game of kicking a ball was a popular pastime among people in Japanese high society in the tenth and eleventh centuries. Later, it came to be played even among people of lower classes.

5. No dance...It is an art form of dance-drama using masks with very subtle expressions. It was developed and perfected in the Muromachi Era (1338–1573).

6. *Oi-matsu*...Literally, it means "old pine tree." It is a tune for No dance that is very slow in tempo.

7. *Takasago*...Another tune for No dance, with a very quick tempo.

8. Musashi speaks again of the absurdity of holding a sword in a specific way. There are some repetitions throughout the book, although it does not diminish the value of the book. When one comes to think of it, it is very impressive to note that Musashi sat down and took a brushpen and wrote the book as he willed. He did not enjoy an opportunity for a draft writing or editing. His analytical mind is obvious as well as his ability to systematize his thoughts.

9. From a standpoint of education in its truest form, Musashi's absolute consideration for the individuality of each student sounds very plausible, although it may not be too practical in modern days.

1. *Kū*...Literally, it means "air," "nothingness," "void," "sky," and "emptiness." But, Musashi's meaning has a positive connotation, pointing to a realm of highest human achievement. That is why it is absolutely more appropriate to use such words as "infinity," "the ultimate," "boundlessness," and "limitlessness."

2. It must be realized, too, that Musashi might have been forced to engage in some combats against his will, not necessarily deadly, for the sake of honor as well as for the demonstration of his ability.

3. *Mu*...It denotes "nothingness." *Mu-shin*, *shin* meaning "mind," denotes "the mind of nothingness," which is the mental state held by an enlightened practitioner of Zen.

HOKKAIDO

Sea of Japan

HONSHU

2
1
4
5
10 3 6, 7
8

9

11

SHIKOKU

12

Pacific Ocean

KYUSHU

0   250 km

MAP OF JAPAN
Marking lands in the life of Miyamoto Musashi

LEGEND TO THE MAP OF JAPAN

1. **Province of Harima** (presently Okayama and Hyogo Prefectures)—
   Musashi's birthplace and site of Musashi's first duel—Musashi was
   born in 1584 in Miyamoto Mura (village) in the province of
   Harima. In 1596 at the age of 13, Musashi won his first life and
   death combat here against the samurai named Arima Kihei of the
   Shinto-ryu style.

2. **Province of Tajima** (presently Hyogo Prefecture)—This is the site
   of Musashi's second duel at the age of sixteen against the samurai
   named Akiyama.

3. and 4.
   Osaka-Jo (Osaka Castle) and **Sekigahara** ("Barrier in the Field")—
   Once the mightiest fortress in Japan, Osaka Castle was built in 1583
   by Toyotomi Hideyoshi and was home to the Toyotomi family, who
   ruled Japan from 1590 to 1600. Until Toyotomi Hideyoshi's death
   in 1598, Tokugawa Ieyasu was loyal to Hideyoshi and was his most
   powerful *daiymo* (territorial lord). However, after Hideyoshi's death,
   Ieyasu quickly broke his written oath of loyalty to Hideyoshi's infant
   son and successor, Hideyori. In 1600, Tokugawa Ieyasu took control of Japan in the historic Battle of Sekigahara, essentially ending
   100 years of civil war, although Hideyori and his supporters—many
   of whom were *ronin* (masterless samurai)—still maintained a

stronghold in the mighty Osaka Castle. With 160,000 men participating in the Battle of Sekigahara, it was the largest battle in Japanese history, though it lasted only six hours. The battle took place at the barrier (*seki*) station for inspection on the main road, which joined Edo (Tokyo) to Kyoto and Osaka. Many years later, Ieyasu finally defeated Hideyori and the remaining Toyotomi forces in two separate attacks on Osaka Castle, thus completing the reunification of Japan. Unfortunately, when Musashi entered the civil war in 1600, he fought on the side that was defeated by Tokugawa Ieyasu. In 1603, Ieyasu became the first shogun of the Tokugawa government, which reigned over a peaceful Japan until 1868.

5. **Kyoto** ("Capital City")—Musashi's combat against the Yoshioka family took place in Kyoto in 1604. His victory over this well-known samurai clan brought Musashi immediate fame. Kyoto was the capital of Japan during Musashi's lifetime.

6. **City of Nara**—After leaving Kyoto, Musashi came to Nara, located 42 km south of Kyoto. Here, Musashi met and defeated Ozoin Doei, the master of spear fighting, killing him with his short sword.

7. **Province of Iga** (presently Mi-e Prefecture)—Slightly east of Nara is Iga where Musashi challenged and killed the master of the sickle-chain, Shishido Baiken, in formal combat in 1608.

8. **Edo** (presently Tokyo)—After leaving Iga, Musashi came to Edo to seek employment as an official Kendo Instructor to the Shogun. During this time, Musashi engaged in many practice combats with many accomplished martial artists, such as a samurai named Muso Gon-no-suke (founder of *Shinto-Muso-ryu Jo jitsu*) and a samurai named Ose of Yagyu Clan. Musashi never lost once.

9. **Funa Jima** (Funa Island, renamed Gan-ryu Jima)—A tiny island located between the north shore of Kyushu Island and the south shore of Honshu Island, Funa Jima is where Musashi's historic duel with Sasaki Kojiro (founder of the *Gan-ryu* style) took place in 1612. After Musashi defeated Kojiro, this island was renamed Gan-ryu Jima is honor of the loser.

10. **Himeji-Jo** (Himeji Castle)—Located about 80 km west of Osaka in the town of Himeji, Musashi stayed here at the age of 38 and 39. First built in the 16th century and later expanded, Himeji castle is considered one of Japan's finest castles.

11. **Kokura-Jo** (Kokura Castle)—Located on the northern tip of Kyushu Island, Musashi stayed here as the guest of Lord Ogasawara in 1635 at age 51.

12. **Kumamoto-Jo** (Kumamoto Castle)—Once located in the province of Higo on the western side of Kyushu Island, Kumamoto Castle is now in Kumamoto Prefecture. Musashi stayed here at the age of 57 as a special guest retainer to Lord Tadatoshi, the head of the Hosokawa family. One year after Musashi's joined the Hosokawa family, Lord Tadatoshi died.

    Reigen-do—Reigen-do is a cave located near Kumamoto Castle. Musashi stayed and meditated in Reigen-do until his death in 1645. During this time, he wrote *Gorin no sho* (*The Book of Five Rings*). He began writing *Gorin no sho* on October 10, 1643 and completed it on May 12, 1645. One week later Musashi died as he meditated in the cave.

    Mount Iwato—Reigen-do is located in Mt. Iwato. Musashi states that he climbed this mountain before beginning to write *The Book of Five Rings.*

BIBLIOGRAPHY

Ichikawa, Kakuji. *Sword of Niten-Ichi-ryu and Golin no sho.*
    Tokyo: Tsuchiya Shoten, 1987.

Ikeba, Shotaro, and Sohachi Yamaoka. *Stories of Japanese Warriors.*
    Tokyo: Asahi Shinbun Sha, 1962.

Kuwata, Tadachika. *Introduction to Gorin no sho.*
    Tokyo: Nihon Bungeisha, 1986.

Matsunaga, Yoshihiro. *A Story of Miyamoto Musashi.*
    Tokyo: Bunka Shinsho, 1970.

Ogiwara, Hiroo. *Miyamoto Musashi: Secrets of the Sword Saint.*
    Tokyo: Kosaido, 1984.

Smith, Robert J., and Richard K. Beardsley. *Japanese Culture.*
    Chicago: Aldine Publishing Company, 1962.

Suzuki, Daisetsu. *Zen and Japanese Culture.*
    New York: Princeton University Press, 1959.

Varley, H. Paul. *Samurai.*
    New York: Delacorte Press, 1970.

TRANSLATOR'S POSTSCRIPT

Translating a work from one language to another is no easy task by any means. From Japanese to English, especially, one main problem is obviously the fact that they do not share the same etymological roots. In the case of Miyamoto Musashi's writing, an additional difficulty is that it was written in the middle of the seventeenth century, and the Japanese language then was different from that of the present day. Compared to similar writings by other sword fighters in the same era, Musashi's writing is clearer and easier to understand. But still, some difficulty exists. One must be faithful to Musashi's thoughts, intentions, and philosophy, which he attempts to describe in the book, and yet a direct translation to English would not, in places, make any sense at all.

In expressing some Japanese words, I have used hyphens to separate the vowel sounds so that it may help non-Japanese-speaking readers to identify and pronounce more readily in the Japanese way. For example, *ki-ai* can be written simply *kiai*, but I thought that a hyphen would help the reader to pronounce it as "key-eye." The name of a prefecture, *Mie*, is another example. I separated it by a hyphen so that it can be properly pronounced as *Mi-e* (*"Me-e"*).

It is my humble and sincere hope that I have contributed even a little toward the understanding of this precious gift from a great samurai who lived his whole life in order to discover and actualize something eternally applicable to a meaningful human life. As for me personally, I will continue to study and train myself so that I may become able to see the ultimate teaching of Miyamoto Musashi, which is summarized in the book of *Kū*.

In preparation for publishing this book, my sister, Hisae Ochiai, and her husband, Hideo, helped me a great deal by giving me advice and encouragement on all aspects of the book. I cannot thank them enough for their generosity and kindness. Jocelyn Fansler worked hard to locate and secure reproduction rights for the artwork and photographs from sources in different parts of the world. I also extend my sincere gratitude to Mr. T. Mikami for his wisdom and guidance, which helped me to formulate this work.